TEACHER'S PET PUBLICATIONS

PUZZLE PACK
for
A Day No Pigs Would Die
based on the book by
Robert Newton Peck

Written by
William T. Collins

© 2005 Teacher's Pet Publications
All Rights Reserved

The materials in this packet are copyrighted
by Teacher's Pet Publications, Inc.

These pages may be duplicated by the purchaser
for use in the purchaser's own classroom.

Copying any of these materials and distributing them
for any other purpose is a violation of the copyright laws.

© 2005 Teacher's Pet Publications, Inc.
www.tpet.com

INTRODUCTION

If you already own the LitPlan for this title, this Puzzle Pack will refresh your Unit Resource Materials and Vocabulary Resource Materials sections plus give you additional materials you can substitute into the tests. If you do not already have a complete LitPlan, these pages will give you some supplemental materials to use with your own plan. There are two main groups of materials: one set for unit words (such as characters' names, symbols, places, etc.) and one set for vocabulary words associated with the book.

WORD LIST

There is a word list for both the unit words and the vocabulary words. These lists show you which words are being used in the materials and the clues or definitions being used for those words. You may want to give students a word list with clues/definitions to help them, or you may want students to only have a word list (without clues/definitions) if you want them to work a little harder. Both are available for duplication. The word lists can also be your "calling key" for the bingo games.

FILL IN THE BLANK AND MATCHING

There are 4 each of the fill in the blank and matching worksheets for both the unit and vocabulary words. These pages can be used either as extra worksheets for students or as objective parts of a unit test. They can be done individually if students need extra help or as a whole class activity to review the material covered.

MAGIC SQUARES

The magic squares not only reinforce the material covered but also work on reasoning and math skills. Many teachers have told us that their students really enjoy doing these!

WORD SEARCH PUZZLES

The word search words go in all directions, as indicated on your answer keys. Two of the word search puzzles have the clues listed rather than the words. This makes the puzzle a little more difficult, but it reinforces the material better. Two word search puzzles have words only for students who find the clue puzzles too difficult.

CROSSWORD PUZZLES

Both unit and vocabulary word sections have 4 crossword puzzles.

BINGO CARDS

There are 32 individual bingo cards for the unit words and 32 individual bingo cards for the vocabulary words. You can use your word list as a "call list," calling the words at random and marking them off of your list as you go, or you could use the flash cards by cutting them apart and drawing the words at random from a hat (or box or whatever). To make a better review, you might ask for the definition and spelling of each word as you call it out–or you could call out the definitions and have students tell you the words they need to look for on the puzzle.

JUGGLE LETTERS

The vocabulary juggle letter game is intended to help students learn the spellings of the words. One sheet has the definitions listed on it as an extra help for students who need it or to reinforce the definitions if you choose to do so.

FLASH CARDS

We've included a set of vocabulary flash cards you can duplicate, cut, and fold for your students. Some teachers make a few sets for general use by the class; others make a set for each student. Some teachers duplicate them for each student and have the students cut & fold their own. You can cut out just the words and put them in a hat, have each student pick out one word and write the definition and a sentence for that word. Students then swap words and papers, with the next student adding a sentence of his own under the last one. You can have students swap as many times as you like. Each time the student will read the sentences written prior to his own and then add a sentence. You can cut out the words and definitions separately and play "I Have; Who Has?" Each student in the room draws a word and definition. The first student says, "I have (the name of the word). Who has the definition?" The student with the definition reads it then says, "I have (the name of the vocabulary word she has). Who has the definition?" The round continues until all words and definitions have been given.

Day No Pigs Would Die Unit Word List

No.	Word	Clue/Definition
1.	ALLEN	Rob thought Ethan_____was a baseball team captain
2.	APRON	Rob delivered her calf
3.	ARM	Injured when Rob helped Apron
4.	BAPTIST	Aunt Matty and the Tanners religion
5.	BARREN	Pinky's condition
6.	BASCOM	Iris_____giggled in the dark with the hired man
7.	BIB	One of Apron's calves
8.	BOB	Born due to Rob's efforts
9.	BROOD	Pinky was intended to be a _____sow
10.	BUTCHER	Mr. Peck's occupation
11.	CARRIE	Aunt_____thought the Widow Bascom was shameful
12.	COOLIDGE	U.S. President at time of novel; Calvin_____
13.	COTTONTAIL	The hawk caught it
14.	DAISY	The Peck's cow
15.	DIAGRAM	Ron didn't know how to do this
16.	DOUBLEDAY	Rob put Abner_____'s name on his test
17.	GOITER	Rob removed one from Apron's throat
18.	GREEMOBYS	Local baseball team
19.	HILLMAN	Mrs.____came to the Pecks for help
20.	HOLSTEIN	Apron's type of cow
21.	HUE	Uncle___was married to Aunt Matty
22.	HUSSY	Died after run-in with a weasel
23.	JACOB	Ran through the Widow Bascom's strawberry patch;_____Henry
24.	LEARNING	Town near the Peck farm
25.	LONG	Ira____ brought his dog to get weaseled
26.	MAJOR	Rob was named after_____Roger
27.	MALCOM	Miss____laughed at Rob's confusion
28.	MAMA	Sewed up Rob's injured arm
29.	MATTY	Aunt_____tried to teach Rob some grammar
30.	NEWTON	Robert_____Peck; narrator
31.	PECK	Pig butcher; Haven_____
32.	PHELPS	Letty_____killed herself and her baby
33.	PIGLET	Gift from Mr. Tanner to Rob
34.	PIGS	Mama didn't mind that Papa smelled like these animals
35.	PINKY	Rob's name for his pet
36.	READ	Haven Peck was not able to do this
37.	RUTLAND	Rob went to the ____Fair
38.	SAMSON	Tried to mate with Pinky
39.	SARAH	Miss____had kittens in the barn
40.	SEBRING	Dug up the coffins
41.	SHAKER	Peck family religion
42.	SOLOMON	The Peck's ox
43.	STODDARD	Poked Rob in the back in class; Will_____
44.	TANNER	Owner of a prosperous farm; Ben_____
45.	TANNER	Mrs.____told Rob to call her Bess
46.	TATE	Rob looked at Becky_____during meetings
47.	TEACHER	Aunt Matty's occupation before marriage
48.	THATCHER	Edward_____made fun of Rob
49.	TROUSERS	Rob used them to help deliver Apron's calf
50.	VERMONT	Setting of novel
51.	VERNAL	_____Bascom died before the novel opened
52.	VOTE	Mr. Peck couldn't do this, by law

Copyrighted

Day No Pigs Would Die Fill In The Blank 1

1. Owner of a prosperous farm; Ben_____
2. Aunt_____thought the Widow Bascom was shameful
3. Miss____had kittens in the barn
4. One of Apron's calves
5. Rob was named after_____Roger
6. Mr. Peck's occupation
7. Aunt Matty and the Tanners religion
8. Robert_____Peck; narrator
9. Setting of novel
10. Rob used them to help deliver Apron's calf
11. Haven Peck was not able to do this
12. Aunt Matty's occupation before marriage
13. Iris_____giggled in the dark with the hired man
14. Aunt_____tried to teach Rob some grammar
15. Pig butcher; Haven_____
16. Died after run-in with a weasel
17. Pinky's condition
18. Rob's name for his pet
19. Rob thought Ethan_____was a baseball team captain
20. Sewed up Rob's injured arm

Day No Pigs Would Die Fill In The Blank 1 Answer Key

TANNER	1. Owner of a prosperous farm; Ben_____
CARRIE	2. Aunt_____thought the Widow Bascom was shameful
SARAH	3. Miss____had kittens in the barn
BIB	4. One of Apron's calves
MAJOR	5. Rob was named after_____Roger
BUTCHER	6. Mr. Peck's occupation
BAPTIST	7. Aunt Matty and the Tanners religion
NEWTON	8. Robert_____Peck; narrator
VERMONT	9. Setting of novel
TROUSERS	10. Rob used them to help deliver Apron's calf
READ	11. Haven Peck was not able to do this
TEACHER	12. Aunt Matty's occupation before marriage
BASCOM	13. Iris_____giggled in the dark with the hired man
MATTY	14. Aunt_____tried to teach Rob some grammar
PECK	15. Pig butcher; Haven_____
HUSSY	16. Died after run-in with a weasel
BARREN	17. Pinky's condition
PINKY	18. Rob's name for his pet
ALLEN	19. Rob thought Ethan_____was a baseball team captain
MAMA	20. Sewed up Rob's injured arm

Day No Pigs Would Die Fill In The Blank 2

1. Uncle____was married to Aunt Matty
2. ____Bascom died before the novel opened
3. Miss____laughed at Rob's confusion
4. Aunt Matty and the Tanners religion
5. Rob went to the ____Fair
6. Aunt Matty's occupation before marriage
7. Mr. Peck's occupation
8. Ron didn't know how to do this
9. Peck family religion
10. Mrs.____told Rob to call her Bess
11. Pinky was intended to be a _____sow
12. Rob was named after_____Roger
13. Owner of a prosperous farm; Ben_____
14. Mr. Peck couldn't do this, by law
15. One of Apron's calves
16. Ran through the Widow Bascom's strawberry patch;____Henry
17. Injured when Rob helped Apron
18. Local baseball team
19. Miss____had kittens in the barn
20. Rob delivered her calf

Day No Pigs Would Die Fill In The Blank 2 Answer Key

HUE	1. Uncle ___ was married to Aunt Matty
VERNAL	2. ___ Bascom died before the novel opened
MALCOM	3. Miss ___ laughed at Rob's confusion
BAPTIST	4. Aunt Matty and the Tanners religion
RUTLAND	5. Rob went to the ___ Fair
TEACHER	6. Aunt Matty's occupation before marriage
BUTCHER	7. Mr. Peck's occupation
DIAGRAM	8. Ron didn't know how to do this
SHAKER	9. Peck family religion
TANNER	10. Mrs. ___ told Rob to call her Bess
BROOD	11. Pinky was intended to be a ___ sow
MAJOR	12. Rob was named after ___ Roger
TANNER	13. Owner of a prosperous farm; Ben ___
VOTE	14. Mr. Peck couldn't do this, by law
BIB	15. One of Apron's calves
JACOB	16. Ran through the Widow Bascom's strawberry patch; ___ Henry
ARM	17. Injured when Rob helped Apron
GREEMOBYS	18. Local baseball team
SARAH	19. Miss ___ had kittens in the barn
APRON	20. Rob delivered her calf

Day No Pigs Would Die Fill In The Blank 3

_____

1. Died after run-in with a weasel
2. Edward_____made fun of Rob
3. The hawk caught it
4. Mr. Peck's occupation
5. Pinky's condition
6. Apron's type of cow
7. Mrs.____came to the Pecks for help
8. Rob put Abner_____'s name on his test
9. Dug up the coffins
10. Rob's name for his pet
11. Uncle___was married to Aunt Matty
12. Local baseball team
13. Rob used them to help deliver Apron's calf
14. Letty_____killed herself and her baby
15. Ron didn't know how to do this
16. _____Bascom died before the novel opened
17. Rob delivered her calf
18. Pig butcher; Haven_____
19. Poked Rob in the back in class; Will_____
20. Mrs.____told Rob to call her Bess

Day No Pigs Would Die Fill In The Blank 3 Answer Key

HUSSY	1. Died after run-in with a weasel
THATCHER	2. Edward_____ made fun of Rob
COTTONTAIL	3. The hawk caught it
BUTCHER	4. Mr. Peck's occupation
BARREN	5. Pinky's condition
HOLSTEIN	6. Apron's type of cow
HILLMAN	7. Mrs.____ came to the Pecks for help
DOUBLEDAY	8. Rob put Abner_____'s name on his test
SEBRING	9. Dug up the coffins
PINKY	10. Rob's name for his pet
HUE	11. Uncle___ was married to Aunt Matty
GREEMOBYS	12. Local baseball team
TROUSERS	13. Rob used them to help deliver Apron's calf
PHELPS	14. Letty_____ killed herself and her baby
DIAGRAM	15. Ron didn't know how to do this
VERNAL	16. _____Bascom died before the novel opened
APRON	17. Rob delivered her calf
PECK	18. Pig butcher; Haven_____
STODDARD	19. Poked Rob in the back in class; Will_____
TANNER	20. Mrs.____ told Rob to call her Bess

Day No Pigs Would Die Fill In The Blank 4

_____

1. Miss____laughed at Rob's confusion
2. Peck family religion
3. Apron's type of cow
4. Robert_____Peck; narrator
5. Rob thought Ethan_____was a baseball team captain
6. Haven Peck was not able to do this
7. Injured when Rob helped Apron
8. Aunt____tried to teach Rob some grammar
9. Aunt_____thought the Widow Bascom was shameful
10. One of Apron's calves
11. The Peck's cow
12. Rob put Abner_____'s name on his test
13. Setting of novel
14. Mrs.____told Rob to call her Bess
15. Letty_____killed herself and her baby
16. Rob was named after_____Roger
17. Mama didn't mind that Papa smelled like these animals
18. Pinky was intended to be a _____ sow
19. Mr. Peck's occupation
20. U.S. President at time of novel; Calvin_____

Day No Pigs Would Die Fill In The Blank 4 Answer Key

MALCOM	1. Miss____ laughed at Rob's confusion
SHAKER	2. Peck family religion
HOLSTEIN	3. Apron's type of cow
NEWTON	4. Robert_____ Peck; narrator
ALLEN	5. Rob thought Ethan_____ was a baseball team captain
READ	6. Haven Peck was not able to do this
ARM	7. Injured when Rob helped Apron
MATTY	8. Aunt____ tried to teach Rob some grammar
CARRIE	9. Aunt_____ thought the Widow Bascom was shameful
BIB	10. One of Apron's calves
DAISY	11. The Peck's cow
DOUBLEDAY	12. Rob put Abner_____'s name on his test
VERMONT	13. Setting of novel
TANNER	14. Mrs.____ told Rob to call her Bess
PHELPS	15. Letty_____ killed herself and her baby
MAJOR	16. Rob was named after____ Roger
PIGS	17. Mama didn't mind that Papa smelled like these animals
BROOD	18. Pinky was intended to be a _____ sow
BUTCHER	19. Mr. Peck's occupation
COOLIDGE	20. U.S. President at time of novel; Calvin_____

Day No Pigs Would Die Matching 1

___ 1. BIB   A. Mr. Peck couldn't do this, by law
___ 2. JACOB   B. Mrs.____came to the Pecks for help
___ 3. PIGLET   C. Pinky's condition
___ 4. READ   D. Rob delivered her calf
___ 5. DIAGRAM   E. Pig butcher; Haven_____
___ 6. DAISY   F. Gift from Mr. Tanner to Rob
___ 7. SHAKER   G. One of Apron's calves
___ 8. HILLMAN   H. The Peck's cow
___ 9. VOTE   I. Iris_____giggled in the dark with the hired man
___10. VERNAL   J. Aunt Matty and the Tanners religion
___11. ALLEN   K. Ran through the Widow Bascom's strawberry patch;_____Henry
___12. TANNER   L. Letty_____killed herself and her baby
___13. BAPTIST   M. Ron didn't know how to do this
___14. DOUBLEDAY   N. Poked Rob in the back in class; Will_____
___15. BARREN   O. Rob thought Ethan_____was a baseball team captain
___16. TROUSERS   P. _____Bascom died before the novel opened
___17. HUSSY   Q. Peck family religion
___18. SARAH   R. Haven Peck was not able to do this
___19. APRON   S. Owner of a prosperous farm; Ben_____
___20. SEBRING   T. Dug up the coffins
___21. PECK   U. Rob put Abner_____'s name on his test
___22. HOLSTEIN   V. Miss____had kittens in the barn
___23. STODDARD   W. Apron's type of cow
___24. PHELPS   X. Died after run-in with a weasel
___25. BASCOM   Y. Rob used them to help deliver Apron's calf

Day No Pigs Would Die Matching 1 Answer Key

G - 1. BIB	A.	Mr. Peck couldn't do this, by law
K - 2. JACOB	B.	Mrs.____came to the Pecks for help
F - 3. PIGLET	C.	Pinky's condition
R - 4. READ	D.	Rob delivered her calf
M - 5. DIAGRAM	E.	Pig butcher; Haven_____
H - 6. DAISY	F.	Gift from Mr. Tanner to Rob
Q - 7. SHAKER	G.	One of Apron's calves
B - 8. HILLMAN	H.	The Peck's cow
A - 9. VOTE	I.	Iris_____giggled in the dark with the hired man
P - 10. VERNAL	J.	Aunt Matty and the Tanners religion
O - 11. ALLEN	K.	Ran through the Widow Bascom's strawberry patch;_____Henry
S - 12. TANNER	L.	Letty_____killed herself and her baby
J - 13. BAPTIST	M.	Ron didn't know how to do this
U - 14. DOUBLEDAY	N.	Poked Rob in the back in class; Will_____
C - 15. BARREN	O.	Rob thought Ethan_____was a baseball team captain
Y - 16. TROUSERS	P.	_____Bascom died before the novel opened
X - 17. HUSSY	Q.	Peck family religion
V - 18. SARAH	R.	Haven Peck was not able to do this
D - 19. APRON	S.	Owner of a prosperous farm; Ben_____
T - 20. SEBRING	T.	Dug up the coffins
E - 21. PECK	U.	Rob put Abner_____'s name on his test
W - 22. HOLSTEIN	V.	Miss____had kittens in the barn
N - 23. STODDARD	W.	Apron's type of cow
L - 24. PHELPS	X.	Died after run-in with a weasel
I - 25. BASCOM	Y.	Rob used them to help deliver Apron's calf

Copyrighted

Day No Pigs Would Die Matching 2

___ 1. HUSSY
___ 2. DOUBLEDAY
___ 3. ALLEN
___ 4. READ
___ 5. BUTCHER
___ 6. BOB
___ 7. MAMA
___ 8. THATCHER
___ 9. JACOB
___10. BIB
___11. GREEMOBYS
___12. PHELPS
___13. BROOD
___14. SAMSON
___15. TANNER
___16. HUE
___17. VERNAL
___18. HILLMAN
___19. PINKY
___20. PIGS
___21. COOLIDGE
___22. RUTLAND
___23. TEACHER
___24. SEBRING
___25. NEWTON

A. _____Bascom died before the novel opened
B. Ran through the Widow Bascom's strawberry patch;_____Henry
C. Rob went to the ____Fair
D. Uncle___was married to Aunt Matty
E. Robert_____Peck; narrator
F. Died after run-in with a weasel
G. Mama didn't mind that Papa smelled like these animals
H. Haven Peck was not able to do this
I. Owner of a prosperous farm; Ben_____
J. One of Apron's calves
K. Edward_____made fun of Rob
L. Dug up the coffins
M. Rob thought Ethan_____was a baseball team captain
N. Aunt Matty's occupation before marriage
O. Mrs.____came to the Pecks for help
P. Rob put Abner_____'s name on his test
Q. Mr. Peck's occupation
R. Rob's name for his pet
S. Local baseball team
T. Sewed up Rob's injured arm
U. Born due to Rob's efforts
V. Tried to mate with Pinky
W. Pinky was intended to be a _____sow
X. Letty_____killed herself and her baby
Y. U.S. President at time of novel; Calvin_____

Day No Pigs Would Die Matching 2 Answer Key

F - 1. HUSSY	A.	_____Bascom died before the novel opened
P - 2. DOUBLEDAY	B.	Ran through the Widow Bascom's strawberry patch;_____Henry
M - 3. ALLEN	C.	Rob went to the ____Fair
H - 4. READ	D.	Uncle___was married to Aunt Matty
Q - 5. BUTCHER	E.	Robert_____Peck; narrator
U - 6. BOB	F.	Died after run-in with a weasel
T - 7. MAMA	G.	Mama didn't mind that Papa smelled like these animals
K - 8. THATCHER	H.	Haven Peck was not able to do this
B - 9. JACOB	I.	Owner of a prosperous farm; Ben_____
J - 10. BIB	J.	One of Apron's calves
S - 11. GREEMOBYS	K.	Edward_____made fun of Rob
X - 12. PHELPS	L.	Dug up the coffins
W - 13. BROOD	M.	Rob thought Ethan_____was a baseball team captain
V - 14. SAMSON	N.	Aunt Matty's occupation before marriage
I - 15. TANNER	O.	Mrs.____came to the Pecks for help
D - 16. HUE	P.	Rob put Abner_____'s name on his test
A - 17. VERNAL	Q.	Mr. Peck's occupation
O - 18. HILLMAN	R.	Rob's name for his pet
R - 19. PINKY	S.	Local baseball team
G - 20. PIGS	T.	Sewed up Rob's injured arm
Y - 21. COOLIDGE	U.	Born due to Rob's efforts
C - 22. RUTLAND	V.	Tried to mate with Pinky
N - 23. TEACHER	W.	Pinky was intended to be a _____sow
L - 24. SEBRING	X.	Letty_____killed herself and her baby
E - 25. NEWTON	Y.	U.S. President at time of novel; Calvin_____

Day No Pigs Would Die Matching 3

___ 1. SOLOMON	A. The Peck's ox
___ 2. HOLSTEIN	B. Mr. Peck's occupation
___ 3. GOITER	C. _____Bascom died before the novel opened
___ 4. VERMONT	D. Ira____ brought his dog to get weaseled
___ 5. HILLMAN	E. Edward_____made fun of Rob
___ 6. NEWTON	F. Poked Rob in the back in class; Will_____
___ 7. TANNER	G. Born due to Rob's efforts
___ 8. MATTY	H. The Peck's cow
___ 9. PECK	I. Pig butcher; Haven_____
___10. JACOB	J. Setting of novel
___11. HUSSY	K. Aunt____tried to teach Rob some grammar
___12. MALCOM	L. Mr. Peck couldn't do this, by law
___13. VERNAL	M. Died after run-in with a weasel
___14. SARAH	N. Miss____had kittens in the barn
___15. READ	O. Mrs.____came to the Pecks for help
___16. STODDARD	P. Rob removed one from Apron's throat
___17. BUTCHER	Q. Ran through the Widow Bascom's strawberry patch;_____Henry
___18. BOB	R. Miss____laughed at Rob's confusion
___19. VOTE	S. Mrs.____told Rob to call her Bess
___20. MAMA	T. Robert_____Peck; narrator
___21. THATCHER	U. Sewed up Rob's injured arm
___22. DAISY	V. One of Apron's calves
___23. SEBRING	W. Apron's type of cow
___24. BIB	X. Dug up the coffins
___25. LONG	Y. Haven Peck was not able to do this

Day No Pigs Would Die Matching 3 Answer Key

- A - 1. SOLOMON
- W - 2. HOLSTEIN
- P - 3. GOITER
- J - 4. VERMONT
- O - 5. HILLMAN
- T - 6. NEWTON
- S - 7. TANNER
- K - 8. MATTY
- I - 9. PECK
- Q - 10. JACOB
- M - 11. HUSSY
- R - 12. MALCOM
- C - 13. VERNAL
- N - 14. SARAH
- Y - 15. READ
- F - 16. STODDARD
- B - 17. BUTCHER
- G - 18. BOB
- L - 19. VOTE
- U - 20. MAMA
- E - 21. THATCHER
- H - 22. DAISY
- X - 23. SEBRING
- V - 24. BIB
- D - 25. LONG

A. The Peck's ox
B. Mr. Peck's occupation
C. _____ Bascom died before the novel opened
D. Ira ____ brought his dog to get weaseled
E. Edward _____ made fun of Rob
F. Poked Rob in the back in class; Will _____
G. Born due to Rob's efforts
H. The Peck's cow
I. Pig butcher; Haven _____
J. Setting of novel
K. Aunt _____ tried to teach Rob some grammar
L. Mr. Peck couldn't do this, by law
M. Died after run-in with a weasel
N. Miss ____ had kittens in the barn
O. Mrs. ____ came to the Pecks for help
P. Rob removed one from Apron's throat
Q. Ran through the Widow Bascom's strawberry patch; _____ Henry
R. Miss ____ laughed at Rob's confusion
S. Mrs. ____ told Rob to call her Bess
T. Robert _____ Peck; narrator
U. Sewed up Rob's injured arm
V. One of Apron's calves
W. Apron's type of cow
X. Dug up the coffins
Y. Haven Peck was not able to do this

Day No Pigs Would Die Matching 4

___ 1. MATTY   A. Ira____ brought his dog to get weaseled
___ 2. VOTE   B. Rob went to the ____Fair
___ 3. HOLSTEIN   C. Aunt____tried to teach Rob some grammar
___ 4. THATCHER   D. Iris_____giggled in the dark with the hired man
___ 5. VERMONT   E. Rob looked at Becky____during meetings
___ 6. SARAH   F. Rob thought Ethan_____was a baseball team captain
___ 7. VERNAL   G. Mr. Peck couldn't do this, by law
___ 8. BIB   H. Rob delivered her calf
___ 9. GOITER   I. Haven Peck was not able to do this
___10. MALCOM   J. Apron's type of cow
___11. PIGS   K. One of Apron's calves
___12. PINKY   L. Pinky's condition
___13. MAMA   M. Mama didn't mind that Papa smelled like these animals
___14. LONG   N. Died after run-in with a weasel
___15. RUTLAND   O. The Peck's cow
___16. APRON   P. Rob removed one from Apron's throat
___17. BASCOM   Q. Miss____had kittens in the barn
___18. SHAKER   R. Peck family religion
___19. DAISY   S. Setting of novel
___20. HUSSY   T. U.S. President at time of novel; Calvin_____
___21. COOLIDGE   U. Sewed up Rob's injured arm
___22. TATE   V. Miss____laughed at Rob's confusion
___23. READ   W. Edward_____made fun of Rob
___24. ALLEN   X. ____Bascom died before the novel opened
___25. BARREN   Y. Rob's name for his pet

Day No Pigs Would Die Matching 4 Answer Key

C - 1. MATTY	A.	Ira____ brought his dog to get weaseled
G - 2. VOTE	B.	Rob went to the ____Fair
J - 3. HOLSTEIN	C.	Aunt____ tried to teach Rob some grammar
W - 4. THATCHER	D.	Iris____ giggled in the dark with the hired man
S - 5. VERMONT	E.	Rob looked at Becky____ during meetings
Q - 6. SARAH	F.	Rob thought Ethan____ was a baseball team captain
X - 7. VERNAL	G.	Mr. Peck couldn't do this, by law
K - 8. BIB	H.	Rob delivered her calf
P - 9. GOITER	I.	Haven Peck was not able to do this
V - 10. MALCOM	J.	Apron's type of cow
M - 11. PIGS	K.	One of Apron's calves
Y - 12. PINKY	L.	Pinky's condition
U - 13. MAMA	M.	Mama didn't mind that Papa smelled like these animals
A - 14. LONG	N.	Died after run-in with a weasel
B - 15. RUTLAND	O.	The Peck's cow
H - 16. APRON	P.	Rob removed one from Apron's throat
D - 17. BASCOM	Q.	Miss____ had kittens in the barn
R - 18. SHAKER	R.	Peck family religion
O - 19. DAISY	S.	Setting of novel
N - 20. HUSSY	T.	U.S. President at time of novel; Calvin____
T - 21. COOLIDGE	U.	Sewed up Rob's injured arm
E - 22. TATE	V.	Miss____ laughed at Rob's confusion
I - 23. READ	W.	Edward____ made fun of Rob
F - 24. ALLEN	X.	____Bascom died before the novel opened
L - 25. BARREN	Y.	Rob's name for his pet

Day No Pigs Would Die Magic Squares 1

Match the definition with the vocabulary word. Put your answers in the magic squares below. When your answers are correct, all columns and rows will add to the same number.

A. CARRIE   E. HUSSY   I. BOB   M. JACOB
B. BASCOM   F. COTTONTAIL   J. GREEMOBYS   N. APRON
C. GOITER   G. THATCHER   K. VERMONT   O. TATE
D. HUE   H. ARM   L. VERNAL   P. LEARNING

1. Iris_____giggled in the dark with the hired man
2. Edward_____made fun of Rob
3. Setting of novel
4. Rob delivered her calf
5. Ran through the Widow Bascom's strawberry patch;_____Henry
6. _____Bascom died before the novel opened
7. Injured when Rob helped Apron
8. Aunt_____thought the Widow Bascom was shameful
9. Town near the Peck farm
10. Born due to Rob's efforts
11. Died after run-in with a weasel
12. Uncle___was married to Aunt Matty
13. Rob removed one from Apron's throat
14. The hawk caught it
15. Local baseball team
16. Rob looked at Becky_____during meetings

A=	B=	C=	D=
E=	F=	G=	H=
I=	J=	K=	L=
M=	N=	O=	P=

Day No Pigs Would Die Magic Squares 1 Answer Key

Match the definition with the vocabulary word. Put your answers in the magic squares below. When your answers are correct, all columns and rows will add to the same number.

A. CARRIE	E. HUSSY	I. BOB	M. JACOB
B. BASCOM	F. COTTONTAIL	J. GREEMOBYS	N. APRON
C. GOITER	G. THATCHER	K. VERMONT	O. TATE
D. HUE	H. ARM	L. VERNAL	P. LEARNING

1. Iris_____giggled in the dark with the hired man
2. Edward_____made fun of Rob
3. Setting of novel
4. Rob delivered her calf
5. Ran through the Widow Bascom's strawberry patch;_____Henry
6. _____Bascom died before the novel opened
7. Injured when Rob helped Apron
8. Aunt_____thought the Widow Bascom was shameful
9. Town near the Peck farm
10. Born due to Rob's efforts
11. Died after run-in with a weasel
12. Uncle___was married to Aunt Matty
13. Rob removed one from Apron's throat
14. The hawk caught it
15. Local baseball team
16. Rob looked at Becky_____during meetings

A=8	B=1	C=13	D=12
E=11	F=14	G=2	H=7
I=10	J=15	K=3	L=6
M=5	N=4	O=16	P=9

Day No Pigs Would Die Magic Squares 2

Match the definition with the vocabulary word. Put your answers in the magic squares below. When your answers are correct, all columns and rows will add to the same number.

A. THATCHER   E. SOLOMON   I. STODDARD   M. READ
B. LONG   F. MATTY   J. VOTE   N. TANNER
C. JACOB   G. BASCOM   K. SHAKER   O. COOLIDGE
D. HOLSTEIN   H. MAMA   L. BARREN   P. BIB

1. Ran through the Widow Bascom's strawberry patch; _____ Henry
2. Mr. Peck couldn't do this, by law
3. Aunt _____ tried to teach Rob some grammar
4. U.S. President at time of novel; Calvin _____
5. One of Apron's calves
6. The Peck's ox
7. Poked Rob in the back in class; Will _____
8. Apron's type of cow
9. Haven Peck was not able to do this
10. Sewed up Rob's injured arm
11. Pinky's condition
12. Edward _____ made fun of Rob
13. Ira _____ brought his dog to get weaseled
14. Peck family religion
15. Iris _____ giggled in the dark with the hired man
16. Mrs. _____ told Rob to call her Bess

A=	B=	C=	D=
E=	F=	G=	H=
I=	J=	K=	L=
M=	N=	O=	P=

Day No Pigs Would Die Magic Squares 2 Answer Key

Match the definition with the vocabulary word. Put your answers in the magic squares below. When your answers are correct, all columns and rows will add to the same number.

A. THATCHER
B. LONG
C. JACOB
D. HOLSTEIN
E. SOLOMON
F. MATTY
G. BASCOM
H. MAMA
I. STODDARD
J. VOTE
K. SHAKER
L. BARREN
M. READ
N. TANNER
O. COOLIDGE
P. BIB

1. Ran through the Widow Bascom's strawberry patch; _____ Henry
2. Mr. Peck couldn't do this, by law
3. Aunt _____ tried to teach Rob some grammar
4. U.S. President at time of novel; Calvin _____
5. One of Apron's calves
6. The Peck's ox
7. Poked Rob in the back in class; Will _____
8. Apron's type of cow
9. Haven Peck was not able to do this
10. Sewed up Rob's injured arm
11. Pinky's condition
12. Edward _____ made fun of Rob
13. Ira ____ brought his dog to get weaseled
14. Peck family religion
15. Iris _____ giggled in the dark with the hired man
16. Mrs. ____ told Rob to call her Bess

A=12	B=13	C=1	D=8
E=6	F=3	G=15	H=10
I=7	J=2	K=14	L=11
M=9	N=16	O=4	P=5

Day No Pigs Would Die Magic Squares 3

Match the definition with the vocabulary word. Put your answers in the magic squares below. When your answers are correct, all columns and rows will add to the same number.

A. CARRIE
B. TEACHER
C. HUSSY
D. DIAGRAM
E. NEWTON
F. COOLIDGE
G. MALCOM
H. ALLEN
I. MAJOR
J. BARREN
K. HUE
L. TANNER
M. SEBRING
N. THATCHER
O. LONG
P. SAMSON

1. Ira____ brought his dog to get weaseled
2. Ron didn't know how to do this
3. Pinky's condition
4. Robert_____Peck; narrator
5. Rob was named after_____Roger
6. U.S. President at time of novel; Calvin_____
7. Tried to mate with Pinky
8. Died after run-in with a weasel
9. Rob thought Ethan_____was a baseball team captain
10. Uncle___was married to Aunt Matty
11. Aunt_____thought the Widow Bascom was shameful
12. Edward_____made fun of Rob
13. Aunt Matty's occupation before marriage
14. Dug up the coffins
15. Miss____laughed at Rob's confusion
16. Mrs.____told Rob to call her Bess

A=	B=	C=	D=
E=	F=	G=	H=
I=	J=	K=	L=
M=	N=	O=	P=

Day No Pigs Would Die Magic Squares 3 Answer Key

Match the definition with the vocabulary word. Put your answers in the magic squares below. When your answers are correct, all columns and rows will add to the same number.

A. CARRIE   E. NEWTON   I. MAJOR   M. SEBRING
B. TEACHER   F. COOLIDGE   J. BARREN   N. THATCHER
C. HUSSY   G. MALCOM   K. HUE   O. LONG
D. DIAGRAM   H. ALLEN   L. TANNER   P. SAMSON

1. Ira____ brought his dog to get weaseled
2. Ron didn't know how to do this
3. Pinky's condition
4. Robert_____Peck; narrator
5. Rob was named after____Roger
6. U.S. President at time of novel; Calvin_____
7. Tried to mate with Pinky
8. Died after run-in with a weasel
9. Rob thought Ethan_____was a baseball team captain
10. Uncle___was married to Aunt Matty
11. Aunt_____thought the Widow Bascom was shameful
12. Edward_____made fun of Rob
13. Aunt Matty's occupation before marriage
14. Dug up the coffins
15. Miss____laughed at Rob's confusion
16. Mrs.____told Rob to call her Bess

A=11	B=13	C=8	D=2
E=4	F=6	G=15	H=9
I=5	J=3	K=10	L=16
M=14	N=12	O=1	P=7

Day No Pigs Would Die Magic Squares 4

Match the definition with the vocabulary word. Put your answers in the magic squares below. When your answers are correct, all columns and rows will add to the same number.

A. HILLMAN E. DIAGRAM   I. LEARNING   M. NEWTON
B. HUSSY   F. COOLIDGE J. SHAKER   N. READ
C. PECK   G. TANNER   K. DOUBLEDAY O. VERNAL
D. MALCOM   H. HOLSTEIN L. TROUSERS   P. STODDARD

1. Haven Peck was not able to do this
2. Mrs.____told Rob to call her Bess
3. Rob used them to help deliver Apron's calf
4. Mrs.____came to the Pecks for help
5. Rob put Abner_____'s name on his test
6. Died after run-in with a weasel
7. Robert_____Peck; narrator
8. Apron's type of cow
9. Ron didn't know how to do this
10. Poked Rob in the back in class; Will_____
11. Pig butcher; Haven_____
12. Peck family religion
13. Miss____laughed at Rob's confusion
14. Town near the Peck farm
15. U.S. President at time of novel; Calvin_____
16. _____Bascom died before the novel opened

A=	B=	C=	D=
E=	F=	G=	H=
I=	J=	K=	L=
M=	N=	O=	P=

Day No Pigs Would Die Magic Squares 4 Answer Key

Match the definition with the vocabulary word. Put your answers in the magic squares below. When your answers are correct, all columns and rows will add to the same number.

A. HILLMAN   E. DIAGRAM   I. LEARNING   M. NEWTON
B. HUSSY   F. COOLIDGE   J. SHAKER   N. READ
C. PECK   G. TANNER   K. DOUBLEDAY   O. VERNAL
D. MALCOM   H. HOLSTEIN   L. TROUSERS   P. STODDARD

1. Haven Peck was not able to do this
2. Mrs.____told Rob to call her Bess
3. Rob used them to help deliver Apron's calf
4. Mrs.____came to the Pecks for help
5. Rob put Abner_____'s name on his test
6. Died after run-in with a weasel
7. Robert_____Peck; narrator
8. Apron's type of cow
9. Ron didn't know how to do this
10. Poked Rob in the back in class; Will_____
11. Pig butcher; Haven_____
12. Peck family religion
13. Miss____laughed at Rob's confusion
14. Town near the Peck farm
15. U.S. President at time of novel; Calvin_____
16. _____Bascom died before the novel opened

A=4	B=6	C=11	D=13
E=9	F=15	G=2	H=8
I=14	J=12	K=5	L=3
M=7	N=1	O=16	P=10

Day No Pigs Would Die Word Search 1

```
C O O L I D G E S A M S O N B I B L
B D T X M T M I L P A A A T G A N Y
U N R N V J A R E E J P T R P Q E L
T A T E D H L R A C O D H T A Y W B
C L X L A W C A R K R V I E Y H T P
H T T L L D O C N L B S L A L W O V
E U H A C Z M T I J T O L C W P N J
R R U S N Q X N N R H L M H W R S J
M Z S E J N L O G C D O A E X D S N
D S S B N P E M D W W M N R O D T H
Y T Y R D B M R J A C O B O R B O L
Z S A I T A S E A T Z N R E A V D Q
J R X N R P V D P T B H S E S D V
M E V G N R T P A E R C C R G H A L
D T A G H E J I L R T O N V B A R N
P I N K Y N R G M A M A N O T K D Z
D O X B Q Y I S H L L C B T Y E M P
L G H U E P C T D A I S Y E C R K Z
```

Aunt Matty and the Tanners religion (7)
Aunt Matty's occupation before marriage (7)
Aunt_____thought the Widow Bascom was shameful (6)
Aunt_____tried to teach Rob some grammar (5)
Born due to Rob's efforts (3)
Died after run-in with a weasel (5)
Dug up the coffins (7)
Edward_____made fun of Rob (8)
Gift from Mr. Tanner to Rob (6)
Haven Peck was not able to do this (4)
Ira____ brought his dog to get weaseled (4)
Iris_____giggled in the dark with the hired man (6)
Letty_____killed herself and her baby (6)
Mama didn't mind that Papa smelled like these animals (4)
Miss____had kittens in the barn (5)
Miss____laughed at Rob's confusion (6)
Mr. Peck couldn't do this, by law (4)
Mr. Peck's occupation (7)
Mrs.____came to the Pecks for help (7)
Mrs.____told Rob to call her Bess (6)
One of Apron's calves (3)
Owner of a prosperous farm; Ben_____ (6)
Peck family religion (6)
Pig butcher; Haven_____ (4)
Pinky was intended to be a _____sow (5)
Pinky's condition (6)
Poked Rob in the back in class; Will_____ (8)
Ran through the Widow Bascom's strawberry patch;_____Henry (5)
Rob delivered her calf (5)
Rob looked at Becky_____during meetings (4)
Rob removed one from Apron's throat (6)
Rob thought Ethan_____was a baseball team captain (5)
Rob was named after_____Roger (5)
Rob went to the ____Fair (7)
Rob's name for his pet (5)
Robert_____Peck; narrator (6)
Ron didn't know how to do this (7)
Setting of novel (7)
Sewed up Rob's injured arm (4)
The Peck's cow (5)
The Peck's ox (7)
Town near the Peck farm (8)
Tried to mate with Pinky (6)
U.S. President at time of novel; Calvin_____ (8)
Uncle___was married to Aunt Matty (3)
_____Bascom died before the novel opened (6)
Injured when Rob helped Apron (3)

Day No Pigs Would Die Word Search 1 Answer Key

```
C   O   O   L   I   D   G   E   S   A   M   S   O   N   B   I   B
  B   D               M   I   L   P   A   A   A           A       N
U   N   R   N         A   R   E   E   J   P   T   R   P           E
T   A   T             L   R   A   C   O       H       T   A       W
C   L   L   A         C   A   R   K   R       I       E   Y   H   T
H   T   L       D     O   C   N           T   S       L       P   O
E   U   H   A       M     T   N           T   O   L   C       P   N
R   R   U   S       N     N   O           T   O   L   H       P   S
    S   S   E       N     O   G               L   M   E   D       S
        S   B       E     M                   O   A   N   R       T
    T       Y       B   M   R   J   A   C   O   B   O   R   B     O
      A     I               A   E           A   N   R   E   A     D
    R   N   R   R       B   M   R   V   P   T   B   H   S   E   S  D
    E   G   N   R       A   E   R   P   A   E   R   C   C   R   H  A
      T   A   G   E     R   I   L   R   T   O   N   V   B   A   R  R
P   I   N   K   Y   N   R   G   M   A   M   A   N   O       K     D
D       O               I       S       H           L       B   E
L           G   H   U   E   P       T   D   A   I   S   Y   E   R
```

Aunt Matty and the Tanners religion (7)
Aunt Matty's occupation before marriage (7)
Aunt_____thought the Widow Bascom was shameful (6)
Aunt_____tried to teach Rob some grammar (5)
Born due to Rob's efforts (3)
Died after run-in with a weasel (5)
Dug up the coffins (7)
Edward_____made fun of Rob (8)
Gift from Mr. Tanner to Rob (6)
Haven Peck was not able to do this (4)
Ira____ brought his dog to get weaseled (4)
Iris_____giggled in the dark with the hired man (6)
Letty_____killed herself and her baby (6)
Mama didn't mind that Papa smelled like these animals (4)
Miss____had kittens in the barn (5)
Miss____laughed at Rob's confusion (6)
Mr. Peck couldn't do this, by law (4)
Mr. Peck's occupation (7)
Mrs.____came to the Pecks for help (7)
Mrs.____told Rob to call her Bess (6)
One of Apron's calves (3)
Owner of a prosperous farm; Ben_____ (6)
Peck family religion (6)
Pig butcher; Haven_____ (4)

Pinky was intended to be a _____sow (5)
Pinky's condition (6)
Poked Rob in the back in class; Will_____ (8)
Ran through the Widow Bascom's strawberry patch;____Henry (5)
Rob delivered her calf (5)
Rob looked at Becky_____during meetings (4)
Rob removed one from Apron's throat (6)
Rob thought Ethan_____was a baseball team captain (5)
Rob was named after_____Roger (5)
Rob went to the ____Fair (7)
Rob's name for his pet (5)
Robert_____Peck; narrator (6)
Ron didn't know how to do this (7)
Setting of novel (7)
Sewed up Rob's injured arm (4)
The Peck's cow (5)
The Peck's ox (7)
Town near the Peck farm (8)
Tried to mate with Pinky (6)
U.S. President at time of novel; Calvin_____ (8)
Uncle___was married to Aunt Matty (3)
_____Bascom died before the novel opened (6)
Injured when Rob helped Apron (3)

Day No Pigs Would Die Word Search 2

```
P I G S R E S U O R T S I T P A B Q
K J E P T B R Z R N H J Y L F A U V
D U H L N O R N O E M Y A M S R T F
H X O E N W D M P H A N D C K B C Q
S N L H M R D A M J D O C O S H Z
G L Q P A E X R A P O M E L D B E W
A V B L V T A M D R R P B O B M R N
Q Y T I V S E R G I D O O E A A E M
F U P G B O K A M M A R N T R L H G
R V C C Y X T N C L B G V A R C C L
D A I S Y R I E V H E P R T E O T V
X K T T E E H W E I E A I A N M A N
R J T T T F U T R L L R R N M T H L
F A I S A M S O N L J E E N K H T T
M O L K Y W S N A M K V N E I Y D M
G O Y G N P Y W L A T Q N R V N G M
H C A R R I E R H N N C A Q T D G R
Q G N I R B E S R D X P T E L G I P
```

Apron's type of cow (8)
Aunt Matty and the Tanners religion (7)
Aunt Matty's occupation before marriage (7)
Aunt_____thought the Widow Bascom was shameful (6)
Aunt_____tried to teach Rob some grammar (5)
Born due to Rob's efforts (3)
Died after run-in with a weasel (5)
Dug up the coffins (7)
Edward_____made fun of Rob (8)
Gift from Mr. Tanner to Rob (6)
Haven Peck was not able to do this (4)
Ira____ brought his dog to get weaseled (4)
Iris_____giggled in the dark with the hired man (6)
Letty_____killed herself and her baby (6)
Mama didn't mind that Papa smelled like these animals (4)
Miss____had kittens in the barn (5)
Miss____laughed at Rob's confusion (6)
Mr. Peck couldn't do this, by law (4)
Mr. Peck's occupation (7)
Mrs.____came to the Pecks for help (7)
Mrs.____told Rob to call her Bess (6)
One of Apron's calves (3)
Owner of a prosperous farm; Ben_____ (6)
Peck family religion (6)
Pig butcher; Haven_____ (4)
Pinky was intended to be a _____sow (5)
Pinky's condition (6)
Poked Rob in the back in class; Will_____ (8)
Ran through the Widow Bascom's strawberry patch;_____Henry (5)
Rob delivered her calf (5)
Rob looked at Becky_____during meetings (4)
Rob removed one from Apron's throat (6)
Rob thought Ethan_____was a baseball team captain (5)
Rob used them to help deliver Apron's calf (8)
Rob was named after_____Roger (5)
Rob went to the ____Fair (7)
Rob's name for his pet (5)
Robert_____Peck; narrator (6)
Ron didn't know how to do this (7)
Setting of novel (7)
Sewed up Rob's injured arm (4)
The Peck's cow (5)
Town near the Peck farm (8)
Tried to mate with Pinky (6)
Uncle___was married to Aunt Matty (3)
_____Bascom died before the novel opened (6)
Injured when Rob helped Apron (3)

Day No Pigs Would Die Word Search 2 Answer key

```
P I G S R E S U O R T S I T P A B
    E P T       R N   J       A U
  U L N O       O E   M   A S   T
H O E     D M   H A     C K     C
  N L H   N R D A M J D O C O   H
G L P A E R A P O M E     D B   E
A B L V T A M D R R P B O B M   R
  T I V S E R   I D O O E A A   E
  U   B O A M   A R N T R L     H
R       T N C L B G A R C       C
  D A I S Y R I E V H E P T E O T
        T E E H W E I E A I N M A
        T T T U T R L R R N M K H
      A I S A M S O N L   E E N   T
M O L       S N A M K   N E I Y
  G O       Y   L     A   N R   N
H C A R R I E   H N       A     G
  G N I R B E S           T E L G I P
```

Apron's type of cow (8)
Aunt Matty and the Tanners religion (7)
Aunt Matty's occupation before marriage (7)
Aunt_____thought the Widow Bascom was shameful (6)
Aunt_____tried to teach Rob some grammar (5)
Born due to Rob's efforts (3)
Died after run-in with a weasel (5)
Dug up the coffins (7)
Edward_____made fun of Rob (8)
Gift from Mr. Tanner to Rob (6)
Haven Peck was not able to do this (4)
Ira____ brought his dog to get weaseled (4)
Iris_____giggled in the dark with the hired man (6)
Letty_____killed herself and her baby (6)
Mama didn't mind that Papa smelled like these animals (4)
Miss____had kittens in the barn (5)
Miss____laughed at Rob's confusion (6)
Mr. Peck couldn't do this, by law (4)
Mr. Peck's occupation (7)
Mrs.____came to the Pecks for help (7)
Mrs.____told Rob to call her Bess (6)
One of Apron's calves (3)
Owner of a prosperous farm; Ben_____ (6)
Peck family religion (6)

Pig butcher; Haven_____ (4)
Pinky was intended to be a _____sow (5)
Pinky's condition (6)
Poked Rob in the back in class; Will_____ (8)
Ran through the Widow Bascom's strawberry patch;_____Henry (5)
Rob delivered her calf (5)
Rob looked at Becky_____during meetings (4)
Rob removed one from Apron's throat (6)
Rob thought Ethan_____was a baseball team captain (5)
Rob used them to help deliver Apron's calf (8)
Rob was named after_____Roger (5)
Rob went to the ____Fair (7)
Rob's name for his pet (5)
Robert_____Peck; narrator (6)
Ron didn't know how to do this (7)
Setting of novel (7)
Sewed up Rob's injured arm (4)
The Peck's cow (5)
Town near the Peck farm (8)
Tried to mate with Pinky (6)
Uncle___was married to Aunt Matty (3)
_____Bascom died before the novel opened (6)
Injured when Rob helped Apron (3)

Day No Pigs Would Die Word Search 3

```
C T J W M R C H H S G L C D X K B W P D
O D S A Q X K B K B S O R K B G U J Q E
O H M C C G M I L O P A I X X C T S U N
L O N G D O U B L E D A Y T E A C H E R
I E R N R B B O C D F Q A A E R H A Z B
D W A I B E M K O V S T D N W R E K Y N
G V V R N O E T D B E S T N X I R O D B
E S G B N Q S M O C S A B E C E N R D H
P V W E S I D B O T B Q A R G M P A P H
H B S S Q G N T R B L L P S P A J L I F
E H U S S Y T G B M Y E T A T M V L G Y
L X Y A P O L T A K T S I M R A L E L S
P G R Z N R R N O T C S S P M N N E T N
S A B T J W G I V M A F T O A I Q N T Q
H L A V C A P F M M V K N R S G K E E Z
Q I R V I Z B T Y A R T E R M E Q S N R
L C R D R P C X R J L U Y R G K A W T Q
V J E N K Y S G Z O T C T M N J W R L L
E G N N E L F W C R U H O L H A K K M R
R T X Q P W S G H K K S A M A M L K G Z
M J M R R C T F V J J D E T W N D W Y Z
O R N V L P D O S G G Y L R C D D S L G
N I E T S L O H N C Q R Q J S H I Z F V
T N M P K B N L D C N J G L Q A E M D T
J N M C F H W F P W D G C D D C W R F B
```

ALLEN	COOLIDGE	JACOB	PIGS	TANNER
APRON	COTTONTAIL	LEARNING	PINKY	TATE
ARM	DAISY	LONG	READ	TEACHER
BAPTIST	DIAGRAM	MAJOR	RUTLAND	THATCHER
BARREN	DOUBLEDAY	MALCOM	SAMSON	TROUSERS
BASCOM	GOITER	MAMA	SARAH	VERMONT
BIB	GREEMOBYS	MATTY	SEBRING	VERNAL
BOB	HILLMAN	NEWTON	SHAKER	VOTE
BROOD	HOLSTEIN	PECK	SOLOMON	
BUTCHER	HUE	PHELPS	STODDARD	
CARRIE	HUSSY	PIGLET	TANNER	

Day No Pigs Would Die Word Search 3 Answer Key

ALLEN	COOLIDGE	JACOB	PIGS	TANNER
APRON	COTTONTAIL	LEARNING	PINKY	TATE
ARM	DAISY	LONG	READ	TEACHER
BAPTIST	DIAGRAM	MAJOR	RUTLAND	THATCHER
BARREN	DOUBLEDAY	MALCOM	SAMSON	TROUSERS
BASCOM	GOITER	MAMA	SARAH	VERMONT
BIB	GREEMOBYS	MATTY	SEBRING	VERNAL
BOB	HILLMAN	NEWTON	SHAKER	VOTE
BROOD	HOLSTEIN	PECK	SOLOMON	
BUTCHER	HUE	PHELPS	STODDARD	
CARRIE	HUSSY	PIGLET	TANNER	

Day No Pigs Would Die Word Search 4

```
Z M Y R R D Y X H J P B A R R E N L G C
X R V E U T V H U P I O C V M I E O T
F O X K T T P B E V G T N B T A C A I B
S J G A D V L H R Z L X A K T M V R T W
Z A M H N G R A R K E D V N Y A Z N E F
C M M S T E Q Q N D T Y O S N P Q I R V
V L B S A O F W D S D M T I U G E D N M V
L B A D O P R T L F A N P B F R G O Z
R A P J N N E C O O D T P I R L W T E G
J S T H I G T C C N N L B G O D E G R J
T C I J E V A R K O T G X S O H D D J M
T O S A T L T M M D V N F T D I H G A M
M M T C S S P R A L L E N H L T I R S Y
C G H O L C E S R W A D P O F R L E O V
B T X B O V X Y G J N M O W R O L E L J
B U S N H W S C A C R C T D S U M M O M
H S T M Y S N T I A E S Q C Y S A O M W
G A A C U T B E D G V N Z B X E N B O B
R R N H H K F A M J D V W T T R F Y N S
M A N F R E H C T A H T V W E S L S M Y
B H E C B P R H K V B P Q I J C C O N Q
R M R F L N F E L X N X R R M F C O X R
J F M C X F T R J J L R H Z G L R S X R
J C S T O D D A R D A D Q C A P Q H G S
S E B R I N G M N C W H W M A G X J N Q
```

ALLEN	COOLIDGE	JACOB	PIGS	TANNER
APRON	COTTONTAIL	LEARNING	PINKY	TATE
ARM	DAISY	LONG	READ	TEACHER
BAPTIST	DIAGRAM	MAJOR	RUTLAND	THATCHER
BARREN	DOUBLEDAY	MALCOM	SAMSON	TROUSERS
BASCOM	GOITER	MAMA	SARAH	VERMONT
BIB	GREEMOBYS	MATTY	SEBRING	VERNAL
BOB	HILLMAN	NEWTON	SHAKER	VOTE
BROOD	HOLSTEIN	PECK	SOLOMON	
BUTCHER	HUE	PHELPS	STODDARD	
CARRIE	HUSSY	PIGLET	TANNER	

Day No Pigs Would Die Word Search 4 Answer Key

ALLEN	COOLIDGE	JACOB	PIGS	TANNER
APRON	COTTONTAIL	LEARNING	PINKY	TATE
ARM	DAISY	LONG	READ	TEACHER
BAPTIST	DIAGRAM	MAJOR	RUTLAND	THATCHER
BARREN	DOUBLEDAY	MALCOM	SAMSON	TROUSERS
BASCOM	GOITER	MAMA	SARAH	VERMONT
BIB	GREEMOBYS	MATTY	SEBRING	VERNAL
BOB	HILLMAN	NEWTON	SHAKER	VOTE
BROOD	HOLSTEIN	PECK	SOLOMON	
BUTCHER	HUE	PHELPS	STODDARD	
CARRIE	HUSSY	PIGLET	TANNER	

Day No Pigs Would Die Crossword 1

Across
1. Rob put Abner_____'s name on his test
4. Died after run-in with a weasel
7. Rob's name for his pet
8. Peck family religion
10. Pinky was intended to be a _____ sow
11. Miss____had kittens in the barn
14. Rob thought Ethan_____was a baseball team captain
16. Born due to Rob's efforts
18. Rob went to the ____Fair
20. Rob was named after_____Roger
23. Robert_____Peck; narrator
25. Aunt_____tried to teach Rob some grammar
26. Mr. Peck couldn't do this, by law
28. Aunt Matty's occupation before marriage
29. Rob removed one from Apron's throat

Down
1. The Peck's cow
2. Ira____ brought his dog to get weaseled
3. Haven Peck was not able to do this
4. Uncle___was married to Aunt Matty
5. Poked Rob in the back in class; Will_____
6. The hawk caught it
7. Mama didn't mind that Papa smelled like these animals
8. Tried to mate with Pinky
9. The Peck's ox
10. One of Apron's calves
12. Rob delivered her calf
13. Mrs.____came to the Pecks for help
15. Dug up the coffins
17. Iris_____giggled in the dark with the hired man
19. Injured when Rob helped Apron
21. Ran through the Widow Bascom's strawberry patch;_____Henry
22. Mr. Peck's occupation
24. Rob looked at Becky_____during meetings
27. Pig butcher; Haven_____

Day No Pigs Would Die Crossword 1 Answer Key

	1 D	O	U	2 B	L	E	D	A	Y		3 R		4 H	U	5 S	S	Y		6 C
	A			O							E		U		T				O
	I		7 P	I	N	K	Y		8 S	H	A	K	E	R	O				T
	S		I		G				A		D				D		9 S		T
	Y		G						M		10 B	R	O	O	D		O		O
		11 S	12 A	R	13 A	H			S		I				14 A	L	L	E	N
		15 S		P		I			O		16 B	O	17 B		R		O		T
		E	18 R	U	T	L	A	N	D				A		D		M		A
		B		O		L				19 A			S				O		I
		R		N			20 M	21 A	J	O	R		C		22 B		N		L
		I					A		A		M		O		U				
		23 N	E	24 W	T	O	N		C				25 M	A	T	T	Y		
				G			A		26 V	O	T	E			27 P		C		
							T		B				28 T	E	A	C	H	E	R
	29 G	O	I	T	E	R							C				E		
													K				R		

Across

1. Rob put Abner_____'s name on his test
4. Died after run-in with a weasel
7. Rob's name for his pet
8. Peck family religion
10. Pinky was intended to be a _____ sow
11. Miss____ had kittens in the barn
14. Rob thought Ethan_____ was a baseball team captain
16. Born due to Rob's efforts
18. Rob went to the ____Fair
20. Rob was named after_____Roger
23. Robert_____Peck; narrator
25. Aunt_____tried to teach Rob some grammar
26. Mr. Peck couldn't do this, by law
28. Aunt Matty's occupation before marriage
29. Rob removed one from Apron's throat

Down

1. The Peck's cow
2. Ira____ brought his dog to get weaseled
3. Haven Peck was not able to do this
4. Uncle___was married to Aunt Matty
5. Poked Rob in the back in class; Will_____
6. The hawk caught it
7. Mama didn't mind that Papa smelled like these animals
8. Tried to mate with Pinky
9. The Peck's ox
10. One of Apron's calves
12. Rob delivered her calf
13. Mrs.____came to the Pecks for help
15. Dug up the coffins
17. Iris_____giggled in the dark with the hired man
19. Injured when Rob helped Apron
21. Ran through the Widow Bascom's strawberry patch;_____Henry
22. Mr. Peck's occupation
24. Rob looked at Becky_____during meetings
27. Pig butcher; Haven_____

Day No Pigs Would Die Crossword 2

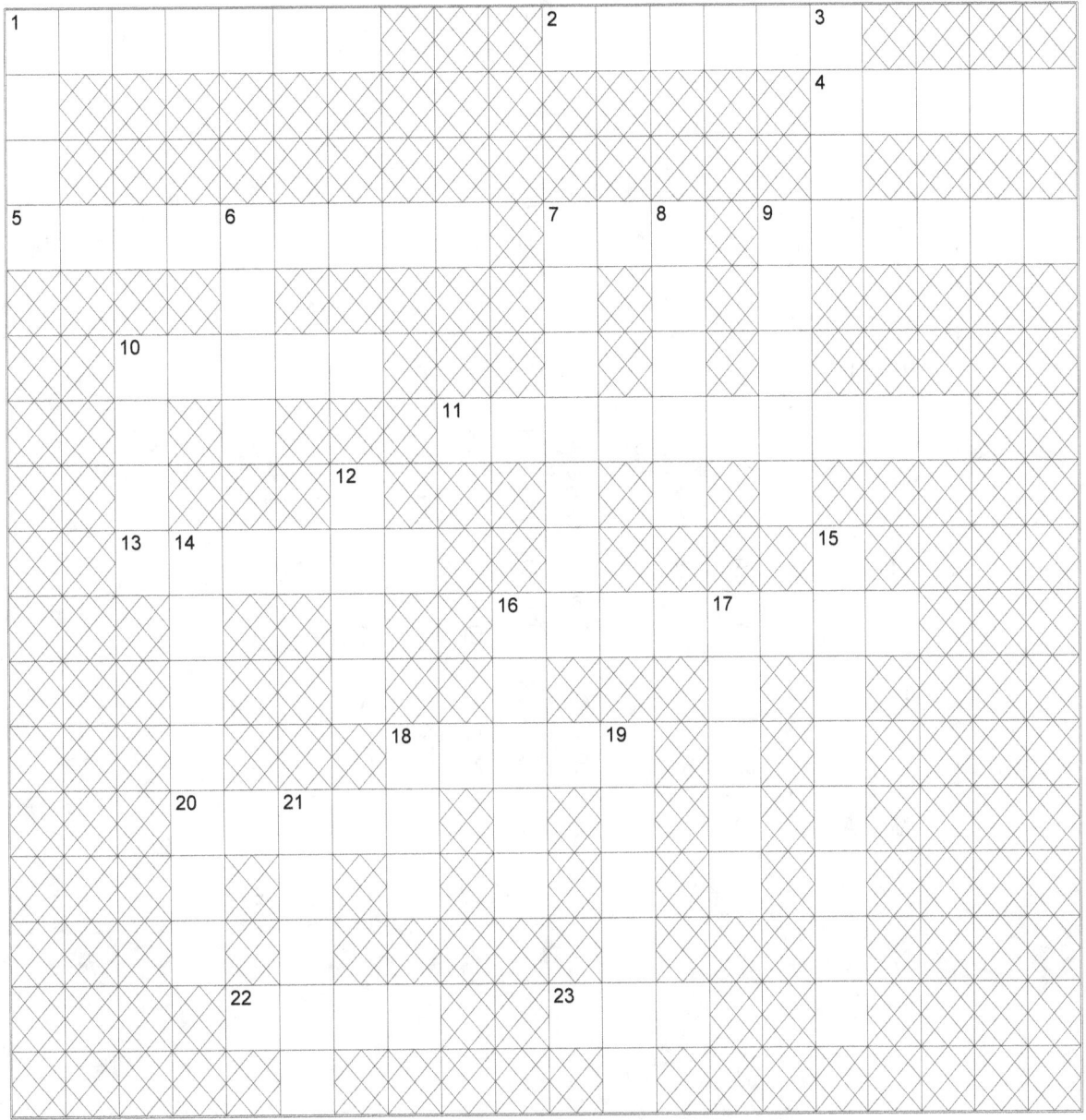

Across
1. Rob went to the ____ Fair
2. Iris_____ giggled in the dark with the hired man
4. Rob thought Ethan_____ was a baseball team captain
5. Rob put Abner_____'s name on his test
7. One of Apron's calves
9. Miss____ laughed at Rob's confusion
10. Rob's name for his pet
11. The hawk caught it
13. Peck family religion
16. Poked Rob in the back in class; Will_____
18. Rob delivered her calf
20. Rob was named after_____ Roger
22. Mr. Peck couldn't do this, by law
23. Born due to Rob's efforts

Down
1. Haven Peck was not able to do this
3. Sewed up Rob's injured arm
6. Ira____ brought his dog to get weaseled
7. Aunt Matty and the Tanners religion
8. Pinky was intended to be a _____ sow
9. Aunt_____ tried to teach Rob some grammar
10. Mama didn't mind that Papa smelled like these animals
12. Pig butcher; Haven_____
14. Mrs.____ came to the Pecks for help
15. Rob used them to help deliver Apron's calf
16. Miss____ had kittens in the barn
17. The Peck's cow
18. Injured when Rob helped Apron
19. Robert_____ Peck; narrator
21. Ran through the Widow Bascom's strawberry patch;___ Henry

Day No Pigs Would Die Crossword 2 Answer Key

	1							2				3		
	R	U	T	L	A	N	D	B	A	S	C	O	M	
	E												4	
												A	L	L	E	N
	A												M	
5				6				7		8		9		
D	O	U	B	L	E	D	A	Y	B	I	B	M	A	L	C	O	M
				O				A		R		A		
		10												
		P	I	N	K	Y		P		O		T		
		I		G			11							
							C	O	T	T	O	N	T	A	I	L
		G			12			I		D		Y		
	13	14										15		
	S	H	A	K	E	R		S				T		
		I			C			16		17				
								S	T	O	D	D	A	R	D
		L			K			A		A		O		
							18			19				
		L					A	P	R	O	N		U	
				20		21								
				M	A	J	O	R		A		E		S
				A		A				M		W		Y
				N		C				H		T		E
					22				23					
					V	O	T	E	B	O	B			S
						B				N				

Across
1. Rob went to the ____Fair
2. Iris_____giggled in the dark with the hired man
4. Rob thought Ethan_____was a baseball team captain
5. Rob put Abner_____'s name on his test
7. One of Apron's calves
9. Miss____laughed at Rob's confusion
10. Rob's name for his pet
11. The hawk caught it
13. Peck family religion
16. Poked Rob in the back in class; Will_____
18. Rob delivered her calf
20. Rob was named after_____Roger
22. Mr. Peck couldn't do this, by law
23. Born due to Rob's efforts

Down
1. Haven Peck was not able to do this
3. Sewed up Rob's injured arm
6. Ira____ brought his dog to get weaseled
7. Aunt Matty and the Tanners religion
8. Pinky was intended to be a _____sow
9. Aunt_____tried to teach Rob some grammar
10. Mama didn't mind that Papa smelled like these animals
12. Pig butcher; Haven_____
14. Mrs.____came to the Pecks for help
15. Rob used them to help deliver Apron's calf
16. Miss____had kittens in the barn
17. The Peck's cow
18. Injured when Rob helped Apron
19. Robert_____Peck; narrator
21. Ran through the Widow Bascom's strawberry patch;___Henry

Day No Pigs Would Die Crossword 3

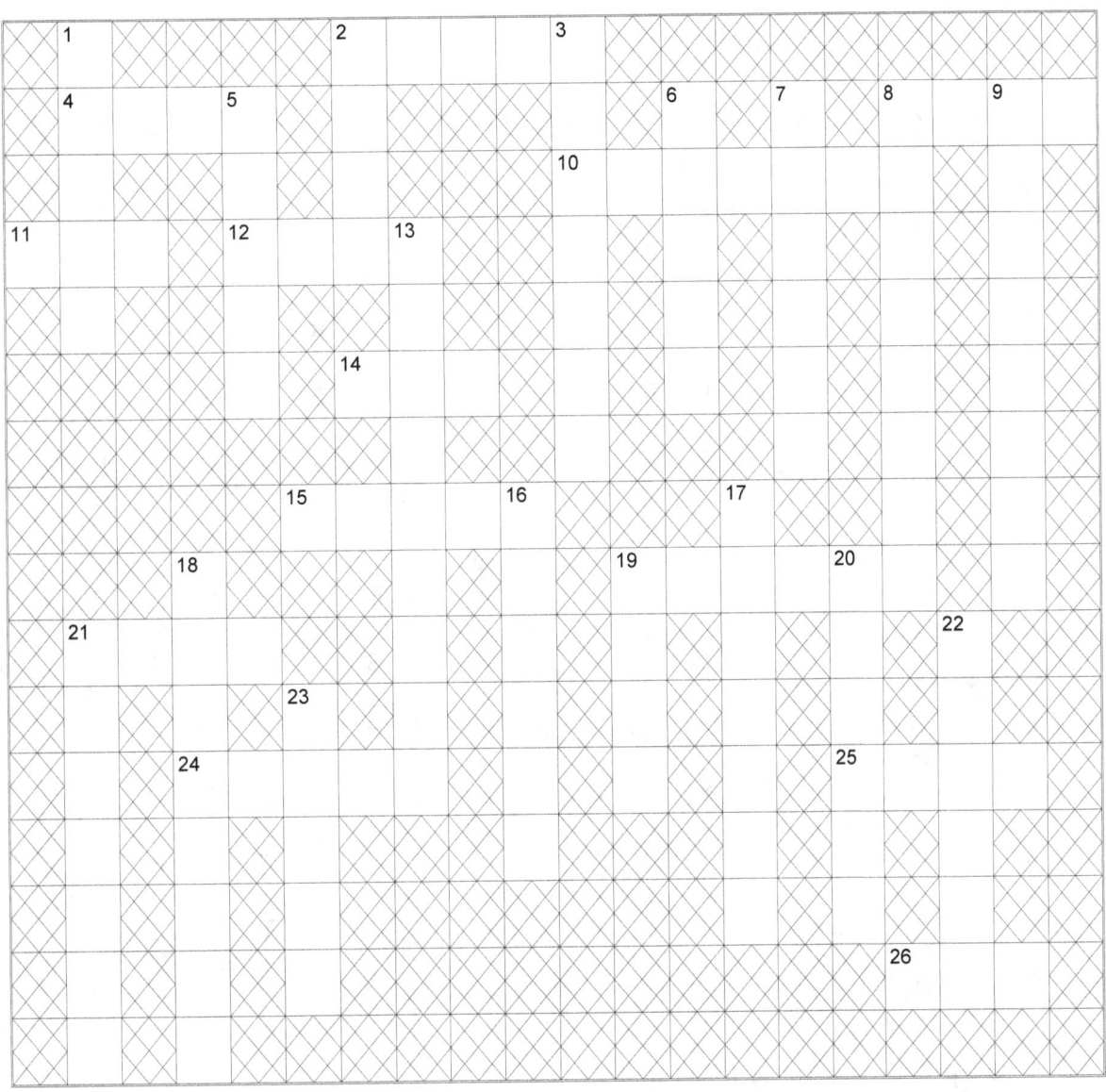

Across
2. Rob was named after_____Roger
4. Mama didn't mind that Papa smelled like these animals
8. Rob looked at Becky_____during meetings
10. Aunt Matty's occupation before marriage
11. Born due to Rob's efforts
12. Haven Peck was not able to do this
14. Uncle___was married to Aunt Matty
15. Rob thought Ethan_____was a baseball team captain
19. Letty_____killed herself and her baby
21. Mr. Peck couldn't do this, by law
24. The Peck's cow
25. Ira____ brought his dog to get weaseled
26. Injured when Rob helped Apron

Down
1. Rob delivered her calf
2. Sewed up Rob's injured arm
3. Rob went to the ____Fair
5. Miss____had kittens in the barn
6. Ran through the Widow Bascom's strawberry patch;_____Henry
7. Peck family religion
8. Rob used them to help deliver Apron's calf
9. Edward_____made fun of Rob
13. Rob put Abner_____'s name on his test
16. Robert_____Peck; narrator
17. Dug up the coffins
18. Poked Rob in the back in class; Will_____
19. Pig butcher; Haven_____
20. Gift from Mr. Tanner to Rob
21. Setting of novel
22. Owner of a prosperous farm; Ben_____
23. Rob's name for his pet

Day No Pigs Would Die Crossword 3 Answer Key

Across
2. Rob was named after_____Roger
4. Mama didn't mind that Papa smelled like these animals
8. Rob looked at Becky_____during meetings
10. Aunt Matty's occupation before marriage
11. Born due to Rob's efforts
12. Haven Peck was not able to do this
14. Uncle___was married to Aunt Matty
15. Rob thought Ethan_____was a baseball team captain
19. Letty_____killed herself and her baby
21. Mr. Peck couldn't do this, by law
24. The Peck's cow
25. Ira____ brought his dog to get weaseled
26. Injured when Rob helped Apron

Down
1. Rob delivered her calf
2. Sewed up Rob's injured arm
3. Rob went to the ____Fair
5. Miss____had kittens in the barn
6. Ran through the Widow Bascom's strawberry patch;_____Henry
7. Peck family religion
8. Rob used them to help deliver Apron's calf
9. Edward_____made fun of Rob
13. Rob put Abner_____'s name on his test
16. Robert_____Peck; narrator
17. Dug up the coffins
18. Poked Rob in the back in class; Will_____
19. Pig butcher; Haven_____
20. Gift from Mr. Tanner to Rob
21. Setting of novel
22. Owner of a prosperous farm; Ben_____
23. Rob's name for his pet

Day No Pigs Would Die Crossword 4

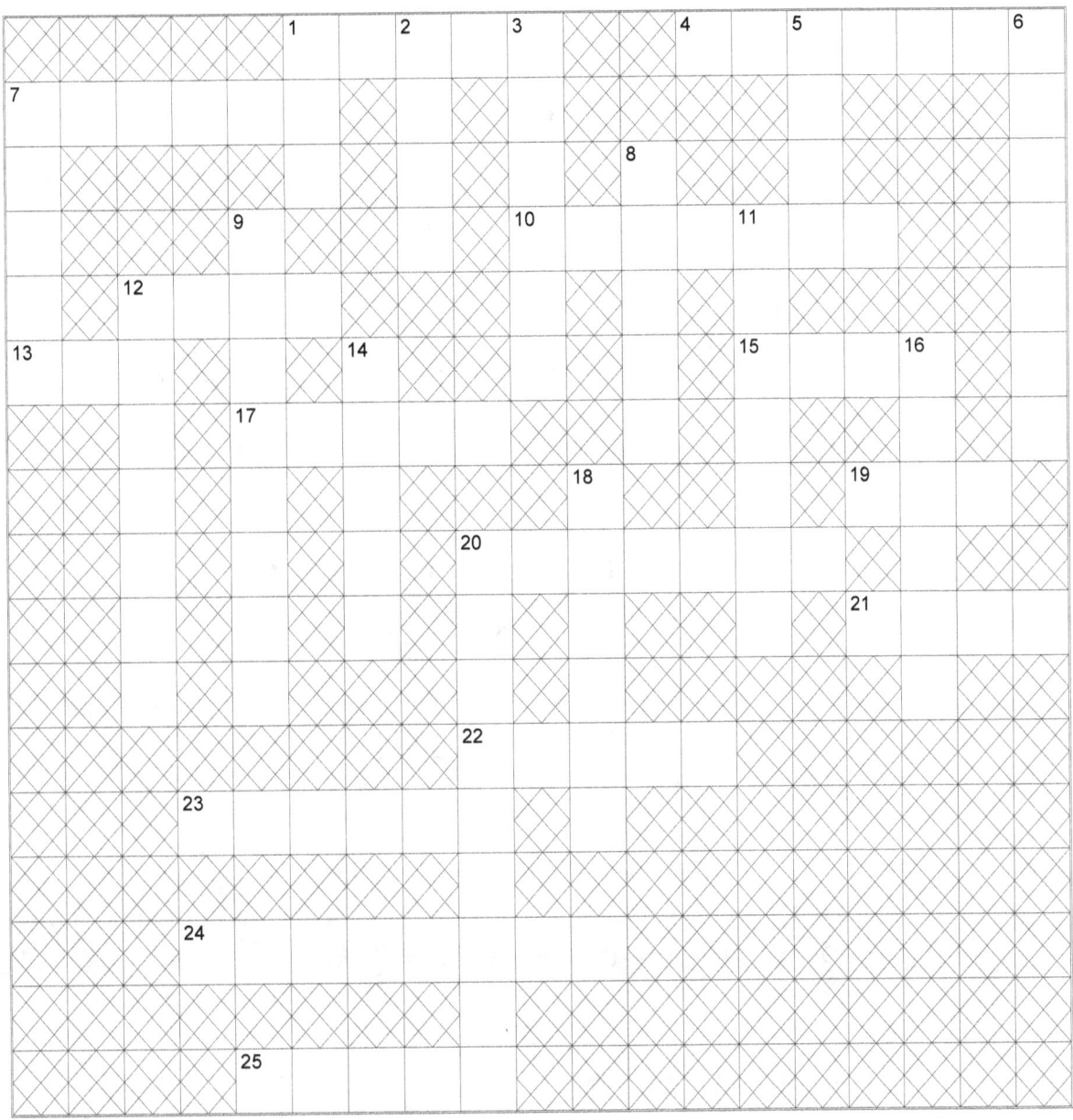

Across
1. Rob delivered her calf
4. Mr. Peck's occupation
7. Peck family religion
10. Aunt Matty's occupation before marriage
12. Mr. Peck couldn't do this, by law
13. Uncle___was married to Aunt Matty
15. Ira____ brought his dog to get weaseled
17. The Peck's cow
19. One of Apron's calves
20. Ron didn't know how to do this
21. Pig butcher; Haven_____
22. Pinky was intended to be a _____ sow
23. _____Bascom died before the novel opened
24. U.S. President at time of novel; Calvin_____
25. Died after run-in with a weasel

Down
1. Injured when Rob helped Apron
2. Haven Peck was not able to do this
3. Robert_____Peck; narrator
5. Rob looked at Becky_____during meetings
6. Rob went to the ____Fair
7. Miss____had kittens in the barn
8. Ran through the Widow Bascom's strawberry patch;_____Henry
9. Poked Rob in the back in class; Will_____
11. Mrs.____came to the Pecks for help
12. Setting of novel
14. Rob's name for his pet
16. Rob removed one from Apron's throat
18. Iris_____giggled in the dark with the hired man
20. Rob put Abner_____'s name on his test

Day No Pigs Would Die Crossword 4 Answer Key

				¹A	P	²R	O	³N		⁴B	⁵U	T	C	H	E	⁶R
⁷S	H	A	K	E	R		E				T			A		U
A				M		A		W		⁸J		T				T
R		⁹S		D				¹⁰T	E	A	C	¹¹H	E	R		L
A		¹²V	O	T	E			O		C		I				A
¹³H	U	E		¹⁴O		P		N		O		¹⁵L	O	¹⁶N	G	
		R		¹⁷D	A	I	S	Y		B		L		O		N
		M						¹⁸B		M		¹⁹B	I	B		
		O		A	K		²⁰D	I	A	G	R	A	M			
		N		R			O					²¹P	E	C	K	
		T		D			U		C					R		
							²²B	R	O	O	D					
			²³V	E	R	N	A	L		M						
							L			E						
			²⁴C	O	O	L	I	D	G	E						
								A								
			²⁵H	U	S	S	Y									

Across
1. Rob delivered her calf
4. Mr. Peck's occupation
7. Peck family religion
10. Aunt Matty's occupation before marriage
12. Mr. Peck couldn't do this, by law
13. Uncle___ was married to Aunt Matty
15. Ira____ brought his dog to get weaseled
17. The Peck's cow
19. One of Apron's calves
20. Ron didn't know how to do this
21. Pig butcher; Haven_____
22. Pinky was intended to be a _____ sow
23. _____ Bascom died before the novel opened
24. U.S. President at time of novel; Calvin_____
25. Died after run-in with a weasel

Down
1. Injured when Rob helped Apron
2. Haven Peck was not able to do this
3. Robert_____ Peck; narrator
5. Rob looked at Becky_____ during meetings
6. Rob went to the ____ Fair
7. Miss____ had kittens in the barn
8. Ran through the Widow Bascom's strawberry patch; _____ Henry
9. Poked Rob in the back in class; Will_____
11. Mrs.____ came to the Pecks for help
12. Setting of novel
14. Rob's name for his pet
16. Rob removed one from Apron's throat
18. Iris_____ giggled in the dark with the hired man
20. Rob put Abner_____'s name on his test

Day No Pigs Would Die

VOTE	JACOB	TANNER	LEARNING	MALCOM
HUSSY	HUE	STODDARD	TROUSERS	SOLOMON
SARAH	PECK	FREE SPACE	COTTONTAIL	MAMA
PHELPS	LONG	BAPTIST	SEBRING	BASCOM
NEWTON	BROOD	VERNAL	SHAKER	HOLSTEIN

Day No Pigs Would Die

MATTY	PINKY	BARREN	DIAGRAM	TEACHER
GOITER	DOUBLEDAY	GREEMOBYS	RUTLAND	SAMSON
TANNER	PIGS	FREE SPACE	TATE	ALLEN
THATCHER	BOB	MAJOR	DAISY	HILLMAN
CARRIE	APRON	ARM	BIB	PIGLET

Day No Pigs Would Die

THATCHER	DIAGRAM	MAMA	ALLEN	STODDARD
RUTLAND	PIGLET	COOLIDGE	ARM	DOUBLEDAY
SARAH	BARREN	FREE SPACE	VERNAL	APRON
PIGS	CARRIE	PINKY	COTTONTAIL	BIB
NEWTON	TANNER	GOITER	HOLSTEIN	LEARNING

Day No Pigs Would Die

PHELPS	SAMSON	MALCOM	SEBRING	MAJOR
GREEMOBYS	TEACHER	TANNER	LONG	TATE
MATTY	READ	FREE SPACE	BOB	HUSSY
BROOD	VERMONT	VOTE	BUTCHER	PECK
SOLOMON	DAISY	BASCOM	HUE	JACOB

Day No Pigs Would Die

SOLOMON	STODDARD	DOUBLEDAY	GOITER	BASCOM
BROOD	DIAGRAM	APRON	JACOB	MAJOR
GREEMOBYS	PIGS	FREE SPACE	VOTE	MATTY
DAISY	MALCOM	TANNER	SARAH	LONG
PECK	TATE	VERMONT	TEACHER	BARREN

Day No Pigs Would Die

BAPTIST	COOLIDGE	THATCHER	BOB	PIGLET
BUTCHER	READ	VERNAL	SHAKER	TROUSERS
PHELPS	CARRIE	FREE SPACE	SEBRING	SAMSON
COTTONTAIL	LEARNING	RUTLAND	HUSSY	ALLEN
HUE	PINKY	BIB	TANNER	NEWTON

Day No Pigs Would Die

COOLIDGE	TEACHER	SOLOMON	TATE	SHAKER
DIAGRAM	PHELPS	ALLEN	MAMA	GOITER
LONG	BARREN	FREE SPACE	APRON	PECK
RUTLAND	TANNER	LEARNING	BIB	MATTY
STODDARD	BAPTIST	PIGLET	SAMSON	TANNER

Day No Pigs Would Die

HOLSTEIN	GREEMOBYS	BASCOM	NEWTON	VOTE
MAJOR	HUSSY	BOB	MALCOM	CARRIE
BUTCHER	ARM	FREE SPACE	PINKY	COTTONTAIL
SEBRING	TROUSERS	READ	PIGS	THATCHER
BROOD	VERMONT	VERNAL	HILLMAN	DOUBLEDAY

Day No Pigs Would Die

ALLEN	VOTE	PECK	LEARNING	JACOB
BASCOM	SHAKER	HUSSY	PIGLET	VERMONT
BIB	APRON	FREE SPACE	MATTY	SARAH
BAPTIST	TANNER	TROUSERS	ARM	SAMSON
GOITER	LONG	HILLMAN	READ	DIAGRAM

Day No Pigs Would Die

BUTCHER	GREEMOBYS	SOLOMON	RUTLAND	PIGS
SEBRING	DAISY	MAJOR	COOLIDGE	BROOD
CARRIE	VERNAL	FREE SPACE	TANNER	STODDARD
BARREN	MALCOM	BOB	PINKY	NEWTON
HOLSTEIN	TEACHER	HUE	DOUBLEDAY	PHELPS

Day No Pigs Would Die

CARRIE	DIAGRAM	HUSSY	TATE	VERNAL
BASCOM	TANNER	TANNER	READ	BIB
SHAKER	LONG	FREE SPACE	SOLOMON	SEBRING
ALLEN	HILLMAN	RUTLAND	PINKY	GOITER
BARREN	TEACHER	GREEMOBYS	MAMA	THATCHER

Day No Pigs Would Die

PECK	HOLSTEIN	ARM	PIGLET	MAJOR
HUE	STODDARD	PIGS	JACOB	TROUSERS
APRON	BOB	FREE SPACE	BUTCHER	BROOD
DAISY	SARAH	MATTY	NEWTON	LEARNING
COTTONTAIL	BAPTIST	COOLIDGE	VOTE	MALCOM

Day No Pigs Would Die

PHELPS	BIB	BAPTIST	MALCOM	PIGS
BOB	PINKY	APRON	GREEMOBYS	BASCOM
SAMSON	TANNER	FREE SPACE	CARRIE	SEBRING
BUTCHER	LONG	MAMA	VOTE	THATCHER
VERMONT	BROOD	LEARNING	HILLMAN	READ

Day No Pigs Would Die

TATE	VERNAL	HOLSTEIN	ARM	GOITER
BARREN	TEACHER	HUE	NEWTON	MAJOR
MATTY	SHAKER	FREE SPACE	COOLIDGE	DOUBLEDAY
SARAH	PIGLET	RUTLAND	JACOB	HUSSY
PECK	COTTONTAIL	SOLOMON	ALLEN	DAISY

Day No Pigs Would Die

BUTCHER	VOTE	HUE	MATTY	BARREN
TANNER	MAJOR	TANNER	VERNAL	RUTLAND
THATCHER	BROOD	FREE SPACE	NEWTON	LONG
VERMONT	DOUBLEDAY	BIB	PECK	TATE
ALLEN	SEBRING	MAMA	HILLMAN	GREEMOBYS

Day No Pigs Would Die

PIGLET	SAMSON	BAPTIST	PIGS	DIAGRAM
PHELPS	BOB	BASCOM	STODDARD	TROUSERS
COTTONTAIL	PINKY	FREE SPACE	ARM	LEARNING
APRON	SARAH	HOLSTEIN	READ	DAISY
SHAKER	MALCOM	GOITER	COOLIDGE	SOLOMON

Day No Pigs Would Die

COTTONTAIL	PIGS	HUSSY	BASCOM	MAJOR
TANNER	CARRIE	PINKY	NEWTON	READ
APRON	ARM	FREE SPACE	LONG	THATCHER
SAMSON	ALLEN	PIGLET	HILLMAN	TATE
BUTCHER	LEARNING	BAPTIST	MATTY	VERNAL

Day No Pigs Would Die

GREEMOBYS	SARAH	BARREN	TANNER	JACOB
MALCOM	BIB	GOITER	HOLSTEIN	SOLOMON
STODDARD	COOLIDGE	FREE SPACE	PHELPS	DAISY
HUE	MAMA	TEACHER	PECK	DOUBLEDAY
BOB	VERMONT	SHAKER	TROUSERS	DIAGRAM

Day No Pigs Would Die

TROUSERS	BARREN	BOB	STODDARD	BROOD
VERNAL	VERMONT	VOTE	PECK	SEBRING
TANNER	BAPTIST	FREE SPACE	PHELPS	DIAGRAM
DAISY	SAMSON	MATTY	READ	APRON
SOLOMON	LEARNING	TATE	COOLIDGE	TANNER

Day No Pigs Would Die

MAMA	BUTCHER	SARAH	COTTONTAIL	SHAKER
MALCOM	PIGLET	PINKY	HILLMAN	DOUBLEDAY
HUE	GOITER	FREE SPACE	PIGS	HUSSY
THATCHER	ARM	HOLSTEIN	BIB	MAJOR
GREEMOBYS	JACOB	CARRIE	BASCOM	NEWTON

Day No Pigs Would Die

NEWTON	PIGS	HUE	LEARNING	ARM
DOUBLEDAY	SOLOMON	COTTONTAIL	CARRIE	VOTE
BAPTIST	HUSSY	FREE SPACE	READ	MAMA
MATTY	RUTLAND	PHELPS	VERNAL	HILLMAN
SEBRING	MALCOM	STODDARD	PECK	SAMSON

Day No Pigs Would Die

DIAGRAM	GOITER	VERMONT	JACOB	BIB
SARAH	TEACHER	APRON	LONG	ALLEN
TROUSERS	THATCHER	FREE SPACE	BARREN	BUTCHER
SHAKER	GREEMOBYS	BROOD	DAISY	TANNER
MAJOR	PIGLET	BOB	COOLIDGE	TANNER

Day No Pigs Would Die

GREEMOBYS	MAJOR	TATE	TEACHER	STODDARD
MALCOM	BARREN	SHAKER	BASCOM	LEARNING
HILLMAN	DOUBLEDAY	FREE SPACE	VOTE	BIB
MAMA	TANNER	PIGLET	MATTY	DAISY
COTTONTAIL	JACOB	ARM	BROOD	BAPTIST

Day No Pigs Would Die

HOLSTEIN	HUSSY	SARAH	PECK	BOB
GOITER	SOLOMON	CARRIE	PHELPS	PINKY
SAMSON	TANNER	FREE SPACE	PIGS	THATCHER
ALLEN	SEBRING	RUTLAND	LONG	VERMONT
NEWTON	DIAGRAM	TROUSERS	BUTCHER	APRON

Day No Pigs Would Die

MALCOM	MAJOR	PHELPS	APRON	HUE
DIAGRAM	RUTLAND	COTTONTAIL	ARM	BROOD
PIGLET	VERNAL	FREE SPACE	GREEMOBYS	READ
TANNER	BASCOM	PECK	LONG	VERMONT
SEBRING	TROUSERS	DOUBLEDAY	BIB	MAMA

Day No Pigs Would Die

SAMSON	CARRIE	VOTE	MATTY	DAISY
JACOB	BARREN	TANNER	ALLEN	HUSSY
SHAKER	HILLMAN	FREE SPACE	PIGS	STODDARD
TEACHER	THATCHER	BUTCHER	COOLIDGE	HOLSTEIN
GOITER	TATE	LEARNING	PINKY	SOLOMON

Day No Pigs Would Die

SARAH	TATE	BAPTIST	BROOD	BASCOM
ARM	JACOB	PIGLET	STODDARD	SAMSON
VERNAL	SHAKER	FREE SPACE	RUTLAND	PECK
LEARNING	BOB	HUSSY	SOLOMON	TANNER
NEWTON	PHELPS	PINKY	SEBRING	COTTONTAIL

Day No Pigs Would Die

CARRIE	HUE	DIAGRAM	DAISY	GOITER
THATCHER	GREEMOBYS	HOLSTEIN	TANNER	APRON
MALCOM	MAMA	FREE SPACE	VERMONT	MAJOR
TEACHER	BARREN	READ	DOUBLEDAY	BUTCHER
PIGS	LONG	MATTY	COOLIDGE	HILLMAN

Day No Pigs Would Die

TATE	RUTLAND	TEACHER	BASCOM	BIB
BUTCHER	DIAGRAM	PIGS	HUSSY	PIGLET
ARM	MALCOM	FREE SPACE	SOLOMON	COOLIDGE
THATCHER	TANNER	BOB	LONG	BROOD
DOUBLEDAY	PECK	VOTE	GOITER	NEWTON

Day No Pigs Would Die

PINKY	GREEMOBYS	TROUSERS	VERMONT	SARAH
SEBRING	STODDARD	BAPTIST	MAJOR	READ
HILLMAN	TANNER	FREE SPACE	HOLSTEIN	ALLEN
PHELPS	MAMA	JACOB	SAMSON	SHAKER
MATTY	LEARNING	APRON	BARREN	DAISY

Day No Pigs Would Die

VOTE	BAPTIST	SHAKER	STODDARD	COTTONTAIL
MAMA	RUTLAND	DIAGRAM	SARAH	VERNAL
DOUBLEDAY	MAJOR	FREE SPACE	SAMSON	SEBRING
BOB	COOLIDGE	PECK	TATE	BASCOM
READ	APRON	ARM	TANNER	PIGLET

Day No Pigs Would Die

BROOD	LEARNING	MALCOM	JACOB	PIGS
TROUSERS	HOLSTEIN	VERMONT	LONG	MATTY
HILLMAN	NEWTON	FREE SPACE	BUTCHER	BARREN
PHELPS	TEACHER	THATCHER	HUSSY	CARRIE
PINKY	GREEMOBYS	DAISY	SOLOMON	HUE

Day No Pigs Would Die Vocabulary Word List

No.	Word	Clue/Definition
1.	ASTIR	Moving about
2.	ASTRIDE	With a leg on each side
3.	BARREN	Not able to produce offspring
4.	BLUNDERSOME	Causing mistakes
5.	BRACE	A pair of like things
6.	BRACKEN	A weedy fern
7.	BROOD	Kept for producing young
8.	CAPSTAN	An apparatus used for hoisting weights
9.	CIPHER	To solve problems in arithmetic
10.	CLERGY	People ordained for religious service
11.	COMELY	Pleasing and wholesome in appearance
12.	CORONER	Public officer who investigates deaths
13.	CORSET	An undergarment that supports the waist and hips
14.	EXHIBITION	A public showing
15.	FARE	To get along
16.	FEND	To keep off
17.	FESTER	Irritate
18.	FRET	To worry
19.	GOAD	A long stick with a pointed end
20.	GOITER	An enlargement of the thyroid gland
21.	HASTENS	Moves or acts swiftly
22.	HUSBANDRY	Breeding livestock
23.	LOCO	Mad; insane
24.	MALLET	A short-handled hammer with a large head
25.	MATTOCK	A digging tool with a flat blade
26.	MIRTHFUL	Full of gladness and gaiety
27.	MUZZLE	The forward, discharging end of the barrel of a firearm
28.	PARTIAL	Having a liking or fondness for
29.	PASSEL	A large quantity or group
30.	PAUNCH	A potbelly
31.	POMADE	A perfumed hair ointment
32.	PROD	To jab or poke with a pointed object
33.	PROSPEROUS	Successful
34.	PROVOKED	Incited to anger or resentment
35.	QUEER	Strange; odd
36.	QUIVERING	Rapid shaking
37.	ROUSE	To Awaken
38.	SHANTIES	Shacks
39.	SILAGE	Fermented green plants
40.	SLICKER	A plastic or rubber raincoat
41.	SMARTED	Caused a stinging pain
42.	SPAR	Non-metallic light-colored mineral
43.	STOUT	Strong in body
44.	SUCCOTASH	A stew of corn, lima beans, and tomatoes
45.	TALONS	Claws of a bird of prey
46.	TRIBULATION	Distress; suffering
47.	TRUNNEL	A wooden peg that swells when wet
48.	VAPORS	Low spirits
49.	VARMINTS	Things that are undesirable or troublesome
50.	YOKE	A crossbar with two U-shaped pieces

Day No Pigs Would Die Vocabulary Fill In The Blank 1

_____ 1. A short-handled hammer with a large head

_____ 2. To solve problems in arithmetic

_____ 3. Claws of a bird of prey

_____ 4. Causing mistakes

_____ 5. Moves or acts swiftly

_____ 6. A crossbar with two U-shaped pieces

_____ 7. Kept for producing young

_____ 8. Fermented green plants

_____ 9. A stew of corn, lima beans, and tomatoes

_____ 10. Incited to anger or resentment

_____ 11. Breeding livestock

_____ 12. Low spirits

_____ 13. Distress; suffering

_____ 14. Not able to produce offspring

_____ 15. Mad; insane

_____ 16. A digging tool with a flat blade

_____ 17. Pleasing and wholesome in appearance

_____ 18. With a leg on each side

_____ 19. A large quantity or group

_____ 20. An undergarment that supports the waist and hips

Day No Pigs Would Die Vocabulary Fil In The Blank 1 Answer Key

MALLET	1. A short-handled hammer with a large head
CIPHER	2. To solve problems in arithmetic
TALONS	3. Claws of a bird of prey
BLUNDERSOME	4. Causing mistakes
HASTENS	5. Moves or acts swiftly
YOKE	6. A crossbar with two U-shaped pieces
BROOD	7. Kept for producing young
SILAGE	8. Fermented green plants
SUCCOTASH	9. A stew of corn, lima beans, and tomatoes
PROVOKED	10. Incited to anger or resentment
HUSBANDRY	11. Breeding livestock
VAPORS	12. Low spirits
TRIBULATION	13. Distress; suffering
BARREN	14. Not able to produce offspring
LOCO	15. Mad; insane
MATTOCK	16. A digging tool with a flat blade
COMELY	17. Pleasing and wholesome in appearance
ASTRIDE	18. With a leg on each side
PASSEL	19. A large quantity or group
CORSET	20. An undergarment that supports the waist and hips

Day No Pigs Would Die Vocabulary Fill In The Blank 2

_____ 1. To get along

_____ 2. To keep off

_____ 3. To worry

_____ 4. A wooden peg that swells when wet

_____ 5. A public showing

_____ 6. A crossbar with two U-shaped pieces

_____ 7. A long stick with a pointed end

_____ 8. An undergarment that supports the waist and hips

_____ 9. Mad; insane

_____ 10. An enlargement of the thyroid gland

_____ 11. To jab or poke with a pointed object

_____ 12. Full of gladness and gaiety

_____ 13. Shacks

_____ 14. A potbelly

_____ 15. People ordained for religious service

_____ 16. Public officer who investigates deaths

_____ 17. A pair of like things

_____ 18. Pleasing and wholesome in appearance

_____ 19. Things that are undesirable or troublesome

_____ 20. Successful

Day No Pigs Would Die Vocabulary Fill In The Blank 2 Answer Key

FARE	1. To get along
FEND	2. To keep off
FRET	3. To worry
TRUNNEL	4. A wooden peg that swells when wet
EXHIBITION	5. A public showing
YOKE	6. A crossbar with two U-shaped pieces
GOAD	7. A long stick with a pointed end
CORSET	8. An undergarment that supports the waist and hips
LOCO	9. Mad; insane
GOITER	10. An enlargement of the thyroid gland
PROD	11. To jab or poke with a pointed object
MIRTHFUL	12. Full of gladness and gaiety
SHANTIES	13. Shacks
PAUNCH	14. A potbelly
CLERGY	15. People ordained for religious service
CORONER	16. Public officer who investigates deaths
BRACE	17. A pair of like things
COMELY	18. Pleasing and wholesome in appearance
VARMINTS	19. Things that are undesirable or troublesome
PROSPEROUS	20. Successful

Day No Pigs Would Die Vocabulary Fill In The Blank 3

_____ 1. To solve problems in arithmetic

_____ 2. Caused a stinging pain

_____ 3. Low spirits

_____ 4. A potbelly

_____ 5. To get along

_____ 6. An undergarment that supports the waist and hips

_____ 7. Incited to anger or resentment

_____ 8. Shacks

_____ 9. A wooden peg that swells when wet

_____ 10. A weedy fern

_____ 11. A crossbar with two U-shaped pieces

_____ 12. To jab or poke with a pointed object

_____ 13. Claws of a bird of prey

_____ 14. An enlargement of the thyroid gland

_____ 15. A digging tool with a flat blade

_____ 16. Not able to produce offspring

_____ 17. To Awaken

_____ 18. Kept for producing young

_____ 19. Distress; suffering

_____ 20. A perfumed hair ointment

Day No Pigs Would Die Vocabulary Fill In The Blank 3 Answer Key

CIPHER	1. To solve problems in arithmetic
SMARTED	2. Caused a stinging pain
VAPORS	3. Low spirits
PAUNCH	4. A potbelly
FARE	5. To get along
CORSET	6. An undergarment that supports the waist and hips
PROVOKED	7. Incited to anger or resentment
SHANTIES	8. Shacks
TRUNNEL	9. A wooden peg that swells when wet
BRACKEN	10. A weedy fern
YOKE	11. A crossbar with two U-shaped pieces
PROD	12. To jab or poke with a pointed object
TALONS	13. Claws of a bird of prey
GOITER	14. An enlargement of the thyroid gland
MATTOCK	15. A digging tool with a flat blade
BARREN	16. Not able to produce offspring
ROUSE	17. To Awaken
BROOD	18. Kept for producing young
TRIBULATION	19. Distress; suffering
POMADE	20. A perfumed hair ointment

Day No Pigs Would Die Vocabulary Fill In The Blank 4

_____ 1. To jab or poke with a pointed object
_____ 2. A stew of corn, lima beans, and tomatoes
_____ 3. The forward, discharging end of the barrel of a firearm
_____ 4. With a leg on each side
_____ 5. To solve problems in arithmetic
_____ 6. A pair of like things
_____ 7. A crossbar with two U-shaped pieces
_____ 8. Kept for producing young
_____ 9. Irritate
_____ 10. Distress; suffering
_____ 11. To keep off
_____ 12. Pleasing and wholesome in appearance
_____ 13. Moves or acts swiftly
_____ 14. Rapid shaking
_____ 15. A plastic or rubber raincoat
_____ 16. A long stick with a pointed end
_____ 17. An apparatus used for hoisting weights
_____ 18. Public officer who investigates deaths
_____ 19. Incited to anger or resentment
_____ 20. Successful

Day No Pigs Would Die Vocabulary Fill In The Blank 4 Answer Key

PROD	1. To jab or poke with a pointed object
SUCCOTASH	2. A stew of corn, lima beans, and tomatoes
MUZZLE	3. The forward, discharging end of the barrel of a firearm
ASTRIDE	4. With a leg on each side
CIPHER	5. To solve problems in arithmetic
BRACE	6. A pair of like things
YOKE	7. A crossbar with two U-shaped pieces
BROOD	8. Kept for producing young
FESTER	9. Irritate
TRIBULATION	10. Distress; suffering
FEND	11. To keep off
COMELY	12. Pleasing and wholesome in appearance
HASTENS	13. Moves or acts swiftly
QUIVERING	14. Rapid shaking
SLICKER	15. A plastic or rubber raincoat
GOAD	16. A long stick with a pointed end
CAPSTAN	17. An apparatus used for hoisting weights
CORONER	18. Public officer who investigates deaths
PROVOKED	19. Incited to anger or resentment
PROSPEROUS	20. Successful

Day No Pigs Would Die Vocabulary Matching 1

___ 1. PROVOKED   A. Having a liking or fondness for
___ 2. HASTENS   B. Mad; insane
___ 3. ASTIR   C. Kept for producing young
___ 4. LOCO   D. Moves or acts swiftly
___ 5. QUEER   E. A weedy fern
___ 6. GOAD   F. Not able to produce offspring
___ 7. YOKE   G. To jab or poke with a pointed object
___ 8. CIPHER   H. To keep off
___ 9. BRACKEN   I. A crossbar with two U-shaped pieces
___10. PROD   J. An undergarment that supports the waist and hips
___11. MATTOCK   K. Rapid shaking
___12. FESTER   L. A long stick with a pointed end
___13. ASTRIDE   M. With a leg on each side
___14. CORSET   N. People ordained for religious service
___15. PASSEL   O. A large quantity or group
___16. FEND   P. Incited to anger or resentment
___17. CLERGY   Q. Strong in body
___18. QUIVERING   R. Moving about
___19. EXHIBITION   S. Strange; odd
___20. STOUT   T. A public showing
___21. PARTIAL   U. Irritate
___22. BARREN   V. To solve problems in arithmetic
___23. SHANTIES   W. Distress; suffering
___24. BROOD   X. Shacks
___25. TRIBULATION   Y. A digging tool with a flat blade

Day No Pigs Would Die Vocabulary Matching 1 Answer Key

P - 1. PROVOKED	A.	Having a liking or fondness for
D - 2. HASTENS	B.	Mad; insane
R - 3. ASTIR	C.	Kept for producing young
B - 4. LOCO	D.	Moves or acts swiftly
S - 5. QUEER	E.	A weedy fern
L - 6. GOAD	F.	Not able to produce offspring
I - 7. YOKE	G.	To jab or poke with a pointed object
V - 8. CIPHER	H.	To keep off
E - 9. BRACKEN	I.	A crossbar with two U-shaped pieces
G - 10. PROD	J.	An undergarment that supports the waist and hips
Y - 11. MATTOCK	K.	Rapid shaking
U - 12. FESTER	L.	A long stick with a pointed end
M - 13. ASTRIDE	M.	With a leg on each side
J - 14. CORSET	N.	People ordained for religious service
O - 15. PASSEL	O.	A large quantity or group
H - 16. FEND	P.	Incited to anger or resentment
N - 17. CLERGY	Q.	Strong in body
K - 18. QUIVERING	R.	Moving about
T - 19. EXHIBITION	S.	Strange; odd
Q - 20. STOUT	T.	A public showing
A - 21. PARTIAL	U.	Irritate
F - 22. BARREN	V.	To solve problems in arithmetic
X - 23. SHANTIES	W.	Distress; suffering
C - 24. BROOD	X.	Shacks
W - 25. TRIBULATION	Y.	A digging tool with a flat blade

Day No Pigs Would Die Vocabulary Matching 2

___ 1. PROVOKED   A. An undergarment that supports the waist and hips
___ 2. CORSET   B. People ordained for religious service
___ 3. ROUSE   C. A perfumed hair ointment
___ 4. SMARTED   D. A potbelly
___ 5. BARREN   E. To get along
___ 6. PASSEL   F. Caused a stinging pain
___ 7. GOAD   G. A stew of corn, lima beans, and tomatoes
___ 8. PAUNCH   H. Successful
___ 9. CLERGY   I. A weedy fern
___10. TRIBULATION   J. Kept for producing young
___11. POMADE   K. Not able to produce offspring
___12. VARMINTS   L. A short-handled hammer with a large head
___13. BLUNDERSOME   M. Breeding livestock
___14. FARE   N. An apparatus used for hoisting weights
___15. CAPSTAN   O. To Awaken
___16. CORONER   P. Causing mistakes
___17. MALLET   Q. Incited to anger or resentment
___18. COMELY   R. Things that are undesirable or troublesome
___19. HUSBANDRY   S. Public officer who investigates deaths
___20. EXHIBITION   T. A long stick with a pointed end
___21. BROOD   U. Pleasing and wholesome in appearance
___22. SUCCOTASH   V. Having a liking or fondness for
___23. PROSPEROUS   W. Distress; suffering
___24. BRACKEN   X. A large quantity or group
___25. PARTIAL   Y. A public showing

Day No Pigs Would Die Vocabulary Matching 2 Answer Key

Q - 1. PROVOKED	A.	An undergarment that supports the waist and hips
A - 2. CORSET	B.	People ordained for religious service
O - 3. ROUSE	C.	A perfumed hair ointment
F - 4. SMARTED	D.	A potbelly
K - 5. BARREN	E.	To get along
X - 6. PASSEL	F.	Caused a stinging pain
T - 7. GOAD	G.	A stew of corn, lima beans, and tomatoes
D - 8. PAUNCH	H.	Successful
B - 9. CLERGY	I.	A weedy fern
W -10. TRIBULATION	J.	Kept for producing young
C -11. POMADE	K.	Not able to produce offspring
R -12. VARMINTS	L.	A short-handled hammer with a large head
P -13. BLUNDERSOME	M.	Breeding livestock
E -14. FARE	N.	An apparatus used for hoisting weights
N -15. CAPSTAN	O.	To Awaken
S -16. CORONER	P.	Causing mistakes
L -17. MALLET	Q.	Incited to anger or resentment
U -18. COMELY	R.	Things that are undesirable or troublesome
M -19. HUSBANDRY	S.	Public officer who investigates deaths
Y -20. EXHIBITION	T.	A long stick with a pointed end
J -21. BROOD	U.	Pleasing and wholesome in appearance
G -22. SUCCOTASH	V.	Having a liking or fondness for
H -23. PROSPEROUS	W.	Distress; suffering
I -24. BRACKEN	X.	A large quantity or group
V -25. PARTIAL	Y.	A public showing

Day No Pigs Would Die Vocabulary Matching 3

___ 1. CORSET   A. Low spirits
___ 2. HASTENS   B. A digging tool with a flat blade
___ 3. PROVOKED   C. Things that are undesirable or troublesome
___ 4. HUSBANDRY   D. Fermented green plants
___ 5. SHANTIES   E. A long stick with a pointed end
___ 6. VAPORS   F. Irritate
___ 7. POMADE   G. Incited to anger or resentment
___ 8. FESTER   H. The forward, discharging end of the barrel of a firearm
___ 9. PAUNCH   I. To Awaken
___10. QUEER   J. To worry
___11. FEND   K. To keep off
___12. FARE   L. Kept for producing young
___13. MUZZLE   M. With a leg on each side
___14. PROSPEROUS   N. A stew of corn, lima beans, and tomatoes
___15. BRACE   O. To get along
___16. BROOD   P. Breeding livestock
___17. FRET   Q. Strange; odd
___18. CORONER   R. A perfumed hair ointment
___19. ASTRIDE   S. A pair of like things
___20. SUCCOTASH   T. Shacks
___21. SILAGE   U. Moves or acts swiftly
___22. MATTOCK   V. An undergarment that supports the waist and hips
___23. ROUSE   W. Successful
___24. VARMINTS   X. Public officer who investigates deaths
___25. GOAD   Y. A potbelly

Day No Pigs Would Die Vocabulary Matching 3 Answer Key

V - 1. CORSET	A.	Low spirits
U - 2. HASTENS	B.	A digging tool with a flat blade
G - 3. PROVOKED	C.	Things that are undesirable or troublesome
P - 4. HUSBANDRY	D.	Fermented green plants
T - 5. SHANTIES	E.	A long stick with a pointed end
A - 6. VAPORS	F.	Irritate
R - 7. POMADE	G.	Incited to anger or resentment
F - 8. FESTER	H.	The forward, discharging end of the barrel of a firearm
Y - 9. PAUNCH	I.	To Awaken
Q -10. QUEER	J.	To worry
K -11. FEND	K.	To keep off
O -12. FARE	L.	Kept for producing young
H -13. MUZZLE	M.	With a leg on each side
W -14. PROSPEROUS	N.	A stew of corn, lima beans, and tomatoes
S -15. BRACE	O.	To get along
L -16. BROOD	P.	Breeding livestock
J -17. FRET	Q.	Strange; odd
X -18. CORONER	R.	A perfumed hair ointment
M -19. ASTRIDE	S.	A pair of like things
N -20. SUCCOTASH	T.	Shacks
D -21. SILAGE	U.	Moves or acts swiftly
B -22. MATTOCK	V.	An undergarment that supports the waist and hips
I - 23. ROUSE	W.	Successful
C -24. VARMINTS	X.	Public officer who investigates deaths
E -25. GOAD	Y.	A potbelly

Copyrighted

Day No Pigs Would Die Vocabulary Matching 4

___ 1. FESTER   A. A digging tool with a flat blade
___ 2. PROVOKED   B. A large quantity or group
___ 3. PASSEL   C. A potbelly
___ 4. BRACE   D. To Awaken
___ 5. STOUT   E. Rapid shaking
___ 6. CORSET   F. To jab or poke with a pointed object
___ 7. CLERGY   G. Kept for producing young
___ 8. LOCO   H. A long stick with a pointed end
___ 9. TRUNNEL   I. Strange; odd
___10. QUIVERING   J. Non-metallic light-colored mineral
___11. QUEER   K. A public showing
___12. BRACKEN   L. A wooden peg that swells when wet
___13. CORONER   M. Full of gladness and gaiety
___14. PROD   N. A weedy fern
___15. GOAD   O. Strong in body
___16. BROOD   P. Breeding livestock
___17. MUZZLE   Q. Irritate
___18. EXHIBITION   R. The forward, discharging end of the barrel of a firearm
___19. ASTRIDE   S. Incited to anger or resentment
___20. PAUNCH   T. People ordained for religious service
___21. MATTOCK   U. Public officer who investigates deaths
___22. SPAR   V. Mad; insane
___23. ROUSE   W. A pair of like things
___24. HUSBANDRY   X. An undergarment that supports the waist and hips
___25. MIRTHFUL   Y. With a leg on each side

Day No Pigs Would Die Vocabulary Matching 4 Answer Key

Q - 1.	FESTER	A. A digging tool with a flat blade
S - 2.	PROVOKED	B. A large quantity or group
B - 3.	PASSEL	C. A potbelly
W - 4.	BRACE	D. To Awaken
O - 5.	STOUT	E. Rapid shaking
X - 6.	CORSET	F. To jab or poke with a pointed object
T - 7.	CLERGY	G. Kept for producing young
V - 8.	LOCO	H. A long stick with a pointed end
L - 9.	TRUNNEL	I. Strange; odd
E - 10.	QUIVERING	J. Non-metallic light-colored mineral
I - 11.	QUEER	K. A public showing
N - 12.	BRACKEN	L. A wooden peg that swells when wet
U - 13.	CORONER	M. Full of gladness and gaiety
F - 14.	PROD	N. A weedy fern
H - 15.	GOAD	O. Strong in body
G - 16.	BROOD	P. Breeding livestock
R - 17.	MUZZLE	Q. Irritate
K - 18.	EXHIBITION	R. The forward, discharging end of the barrel of a firearm
Y - 19.	ASTRIDE	S. Incited to anger or resentment
C - 20.	PAUNCH	T. People ordained for religious service
A - 21.	MATTOCK	U. Public officer who investigates deaths
J - 22.	SPAR	V. Mad; insane
D - 23.	ROUSE	W. A pair of like things
P - 24.	HUSBANDRY	X. An undergarment that supports the waist and hips
M - 25.	MIRTHFUL	Y. With a leg on each side

Day No Pigs Would Die Vocabulary Magic Squares 1

Match the definition with the vocabulary word. Put your answers in the magic squares below. When your answers are correct, all columns and rows will add to the same number.

A. POMADE
B. SPAR
C. COMELY
D. CIPHER
E. CAPSTAN
F. FRET
G. PROSPEROUS
H. SHANTIES
I. VAPORS
J. ROUSE
K. MUZZLE
L. BLUNDERSOME
M. SMARTED
N. YOKE
O. FARE
P. LOCO

1. A perfumed hair ointment
2. A crossbar with two U-shaped pieces
3. To Awaken
4. An apparatus used for hoisting weights
5. Successful
6. Causing mistakes
7. Mad; insane
8. Pleasing and wholesome in appearance
9. To get along
10. To solve problems in arithmetic
11. Shacks
12. The forward, discharging end of the barrel of a firearm
13. Low spirits
14. To worry
15. Non-metallic light-colored mineral
16. Caused a stinging pain

A=	B=	C=	D=
E=	F=	G=	H=
I=	J=	K=	L=
M=	N=	O=	P=

Day No Pigs Would Die Vocablary Magic Squares 1 Answer Key

Match the definition with the vocabulary word. Put your answers in the magic squares below. When your answers are correct, all columns and rows will add to the same number.

A. POMADE
B. SPAR
C. COMELY
D. CIPHER
E. CAPSTAN
F. FRET
G. PROSPEROUS
H. SHANTIES
I. VAPORS
J. ROUSE
K. MUZZLE
L. BLUNDERSOME
M. SMARTED
N. YOKE
O. FARE
P. LOCO

1. A perfumed hair ointment
2. A crossbar with two U-shaped pieces
3. To Awaken
4. An apparatus used for hoisting weights
5. Successful
6. Causing mistakes
7. Mad; insane
8. Pleasing and wholesome in appearance
9. To get along
10. To solve problems in arithmetic
11. Shacks
12. The forward, discharging end of the barrel of a firearm
13. Low spirits
14. To worry
15. Non-metallic light-colored mineral
16. Caused a stinging pain

A=1	B=15	C=8	D=10
E=4	F=14	G=5	H=11
I=13	J=3	K=12	L=6
M=16	N=2	O=9	P=7

Day No Pigs Would Die Vocabulary Magic Squares 2

Match the definition with the vocabulary word. Put your answers in the magic squares below. When your answers are correct, all columns and rows will add to the same number.

A. CLERGY
B. PARTIAL
C. EXHIBITION
D. FARE
E. ASTIR
F. PASSEL
G. BRACKEN
H. SMARTED
I. PROVOKED
J. FRET
K. SUCCOTASH
L. MATTOCK
M. POMADE
N. TRUNNEL
O. MUZZLE
P. BRACE

1. A wooden peg that swells when wet
2. A weedy fern
3. A digging tool with a flat blade
4. People ordained for religious service
5. A stew of corn, lima beans, and tomatoes
6. Having a liking or fondness for
7. A perfumed hair ointment
8. Caused a stinging pain
9. Moving about
10. A pair of like things
11. A public showing
12. To worry
13. To get along
14. Incited to anger or resentment
15. A large quantity or group
16. The forward, discharging end of the barrel of a firearm

A=	B=	C=	D=
E=	F=	G=	H=
I=	J=	K=	L=
M=	N=	O=	P=

Day No Pigs Would Die Vocabulary Magic Squares 2 Answer Key

Match the definition with the vocabulary word. Put your answers in the magic squares below. When your answers are correct, all columns and rows will add to the same number.

A. CLERGY
B. PARTIAL
C. EXHIBITION
D. FARE
E. ASTIR
F. PASSEL
G. BRACKEN
H. SMARTED
I. PROVOKED
J. FRET
K. SUCCOTASH
L. MATTOCK
M. POMADE
N. TRUNNEL
O. MUZZLE
P. BRACE

1. A wooden peg that swells when wet
2. A weedy fern
3. A digging tool with a flat blade
4. People ordained for religious service
5. A stew of corn, lima beans, and tomatoes
6. Having a liking or fondness for
7. A perfumed hair ointment
8. Caused a stinging pain
9. Moving about
10. A pair of like things
11. A public showing
12. To worry
13. To get along
14. Incited to anger or resentment
15. A large quantity or group
16. The forward, discharging end of the barrel of a firearm

A=4	B=6	C=11	D=13
E=9	F=15	G=2	H=8
I=14	J=12	K=5	L=3
M=7	N=1	O=16	P=10

Day No Pigs Would Die Vocabulary Magic Squares 3

Match the definition with the vocabulary word. Put your answers in the magic squares below. When your answers are correct, all columns and rows will add to the same number.

A. FRET   E. COMELY   I. HUSBANDRY   M. BRACKEN
B. POMADE   F. CLERGY   J. ASTRIDE   N. GOITER
C. BLUNDERSOME   G. SLICKER   K. ROUSE   O. CORSET
D. BRACE   H. HASTENS   L. YOKE   P. MATTOCK

1. A weedy fern
2. People ordained for religious service
3. Moves or acts swiftly
4. An undergarment that supports the waist and hips
5. A crossbar with two U-shaped pieces
6. Causing mistakes
7. To worry
8. With a leg on each side
9. To Awaken
10. A pair of like things
11. A perfumed hair ointment
12. Breeding livestock
13. An enlargement of the thyroid gland
14. Pleasing and wholesome in appearance
15. A plastic or rubber raincoat
16. A digging tool with a flat blade

A=	B=	C=	D=
E=	F=	G=	H=
I=	J=	K=	L=
M=	N=	O=	P=

Day No Pigs Would Die Vocabulary Magic Squares 3 Answer Key

Match the definition with the vocabulary word. Put your answers in the magic squares below. When your answers are correct, all columns and rows will add to the same number.

A. FRET
B. POMADE
C. BLUNDERSOME
D. BRACE
E. COMELY
F. CLERGY
G. SLICKER
H. HASTENS
I. HUSBANDRY
J. ASTRIDE
K. ROUSE
L. YOKE
M. BRACKEN
N. GOITER
O. CORSET
P. MATTOCK

1. A weedy fern
2. People ordained for religious service
3. Moves or acts swiftly
4. An undergarment that supports the waist and hips
5. A crossbar with two U-shaped pieces
6. Causing mistakes
7. To worry
8. With a leg on each side
9. To Awaken
10. A pair of like things
11. A perfumed hair ointment
12. Breeding livestock
13. An enlargement of the thyroid gland
14. Pleasing and wholesome in appearance
15. A plastic or rubber raincoat
16. A digging tool with a flat blade

A=7	B=11	C=6	D=10
E=14	F=2	G=15	H=3
I=12	J=8	K=9	L=5
M=1	N=13	O=4	P=16

Day No Pigs Would Die Vocabulary Magic Squares 4

Match the definition with the vocabulary word. Put your answers in the magic squares below. When your answers are correct, all columns and rows will add to the same number.

A. BLUNDERSOME E. SUCCOTASH I. PARTIAL   M. HASTENS
B. QUIVERING   F. YOKE   J. MATTOCK   N. CAPSTAN
C. FRET   G. SMARTED   K. TALONS   O. LOCO
D. BROOD   H. MUZZLE   L. BRACE   P. PAUNCH

1. To worry
2. A digging tool with a flat blade
3. A crossbar with two U-shaped pieces
4. Mad; insane
5. A potbelly
6. A stew of corn, lima beans, and tomatoes
7. Having a liking or fondness for
8. Kept for producing young
9. Moves or acts swiftly
10. The forward, discharging end of the barrel of a firearm
11. A pair of like things
12. Causing mistakes
13. Rapid shaking
14. Claws of a bird of prey
15. Caused a stinging pain
16. An apparatus used for hoisting weights

A=	B=	C=	D=
E=	F=	G=	H=
I=	J=	K=	L=
M=	N=	O=	P=

Day No Pigs Would Die Vocabulary Magic Squares 4 Answer Key

Match the definition with the vocabulary word. Put your answers in the magic squares below. When your answers are correct, all columns and rows will add to the same number.

A. BLUNDERSOME
B. QUIVERING
C. FRET
D. BROOD
E. SUCCOTASH
F. YOKE
G. SMARTED
H. MUZZLE
I. PARTIAL
J. MATTOCK
K. TALONS
L. BRACE
M. HASTENS
N. CAPSTAN
O. LOCO
P. PAUNCH

1. To worry
2. A digging tool with a flat blade
3. A crossbar with two U-shaped pieces
4. Mad; insane
5. A potbelly
6. A stew of corn, lima beans, and tomatoes
7. Having a liking or fondness for
8. Kept for producing young
9. Moves or acts swiftly
10. The forward, discharging end of the barrel of a firearm
11. A pair of like things
12. Causing mistakes
13. Rapid shaking
14. Claws of a bird of prey
15. Caused a stinging pain
16. An apparatus used for hoisting weights

A=12	B=13	C=1	D=8
E=6	F=3	G=15	H=10
I=7	J=2	K=14	L=11
M=9	N=16	O=4	P=5

Day No Pigs Would Die Vocabulary Word Search 1

```
A S T I R K R D E K O V O R P V B H B G
P X X E S E Z D S P P A W E S A J D R B
M A E N T Q I O T Q G P R H M R P P A K
F U U I B R X R T D D O B P A M A R C K
Q C O N T L M P S B X R K I R I R O K L
X G O S C K U I Y S O S C C T N T S E M
K M A R J H L N R O M D V P E T I P N K
P Q V D S A R P D T V T X A D S A E Z V
B F B V G E B D W E H Z F S R L L R G F
L A A E N H T L Y P R F X S C O V O P S
S R R O L Q E R K S L S U E S N U U D C
T E R F E N D S T O U T O L R A P S C F
B O E N N N A M C S B C I M E B N N E K
C C N U A R M O A C P C C L E O G E X M
K P R B E Y O K E L K W Z O L N M T G T
K T S T L F P M B E L Z B A T H F S O K
R U S E Z L K Q R R U E T Z H A Y A A F
H E M C L E R G Y M A T T O C K S H D C
F O Q U I V E R I N G C S W J M Q H K R
C E X H I B I T I O N F E C A P S T A N
```

Breeding livestock (9)
A crossbar with two U-shaped pieces (4)
A digging tool with a flat blade (7)
A large quantity or group (6)
A long stick with a pointed end (4)
A pair of like things (5)
A perfumed hair ointment (6)
A plastic or rubber raincoat (7)
A potbelly (6)
A public showing (10)
A short-handled hammer with a large head (6)
A stew of corn, lima beans, and tomatoes (9)
A weedy fern (7)
A wooden peg that swells when wet (7)
An apparatus used for hoisting weights (7)
An enlargement of the thyroid gland (6)
An undergarment that supports the waist and hips (6)
Caused a stinging pain (7)
Causing mistakes (11)
Claws of a bird of prey (6)
Fermented green plants (6)
Full of gladness and gaiety (8)
Having a liking or fondness for (7)
Incited to anger or resentment (8)
Irritate (6)

Kept for producing young (5)
Low spirits (6)
Mad; insane (4)
Moving about (5)
Non-metallic light-colored mineral (4)
Not able to produce offspring (6)
People ordained for religious service (6)
Pleasing and wholesome in appearance (6)
Public officer who investigates deaths (7)
Rapid shaking (9)
Strange; odd (5)
Strong in body (5)
Successful (10)
The forward, discharging end of the barrel of a firearm (6)
Things that are undesirable or troublesome (8)
To Awaken (5)
To get along (4)
To jab or poke with a pointed object (4)
To keep off (4)
To solve problems in arithmetic (6)
To worry (4)
With a leg on each side (7)
Moves or acts swiftly (7)

Day No Pigs Would Die Vocabulary Word Search 1 Answer Key

Breeding livestock (9)
A crossbar with two U-shaped pieces (4)
A digging tool with a flat blade (7)
A large quantity or group (6)
A long stick with a pointed end (4)
A pair of like things (5)
A perfumed hair ointment (6)
A plastic or rubber raincoat (7)
A potbelly (6)
A public showing (10)
A short-handled hammer with a large head (6)
A stew of corn, lima beans, and tomatoes (9)
A weedy fern (7)
A wooden peg that swells when wet (7)
An apparatus used for hoisting weights (7)
An enlargement of the thyroid gland (6)
An undergarment that supports the waist and hips (6)
Caused a stinging pain (7)
Causing mistakes (11)
Claws of a bird of prey (6)
Fermented green plants (6)
Full of gladness and gaiety (8)
Having a liking or fondness for (7)
Incited to anger or resentment (8)
Irritate (6)

Kept for producing young (5)
Low spirits (6)
Mad; insane (4)
Moving about (5)
Non-metallic light-colored mineral (4)
Not able to produce offspring (6)
People ordained for religious service (6)
Pleasing and wholesome in appearance (6)
Public officer who investigates deaths (7)
Rapid shaking (9)
Strange; odd (5)
Strong in body (5)
Successful (10)
The forward, discharging end of the barrel of a firearm (6)
Things that are undesirable or troublesome (8)
To Awaken (5)
To get along (4)
To jab or poke with a pointed object (4)
To keep off (4)
To solve problems in arithmetic (6)
To worry (4)
With a leg on each side (7)
Moves or acts swiftly (7)

Day No Pigs Would Die Vocabulary Word Search 2

```
H U S B A N D R Y A F B T E L L A M M N
C D E L O X E A D S F E G A T R K X A W
N C K C Z K S P T T S A S S L P Z S T J
U S O Z C P T S P R L M R T Q O E K T S
A L Y I L E O Q O I N I E E I N R O G
P H L S R X U C S D Y B P R T R U S C D
V S L F Y L T D R E Q X U N T N C J K L
B A R R E N E G E S L U A L N H F E N D
Y Y R S S K L Y X U M H E E A C F A M L
P P S M O A W R H O S A L E X T T U S T
W A S V I Y E K I R G G R C R S I N L D
P D O T G N J M B A Q O F T P N E O G R
X R R R O B T R I S S W I A E T L C N W
P A E R L V R S T H G T C T S D Q H I P
P L O Y X F M O I P O Y I A E O S D R H
C C D T S U C C O T A S H R B R A C E W
Y B X Q Z N K M N D D Z B M O P D X V K
N M G Z B R A C K E N L Y P C Q K G I T
Z B L U N D E R S O M E A R B C F F U Z
V E V R E H P I C W J V C O M E L Y Q S
```

Breeding livestock (9)
A crossbar with two U-shaped pieces (4)
A digging tool with a flat blade (7)
A large quantity or group (6)
A long stick with a pointed end (4)
A pair of like things (5)
A perfumed hair ointment (6)
A plastic or rubber raincoat (7)
A potbelly (6)
A public showing (10)
A short-handled hammer with a large head (6)
A stew of corn, lima beans, and tomatoes (9)
A weedy fern (7)
A wooden peg that swells when wet (7)
An apparatus used for hoisting weights (7)
An enlargement of the thyroid gland (6)
An undergarment that supports the waist and hips (6)
Caused a stinging pain (7)
Causing mistakes (11)
Claws of a bird of prey (6)
Distress; suffering (11)
Fermented green plants (6)
Full of gladness and gaiety (8)
Having a liking or fondness for (7)
Incited to anger or resentment (8)
Irritate (6)
Kept for producing young (5)
Low spirits (6)
Mad; insane (4)
Moving about (5)
Non-metallic light-colored mineral (4)
Not able to produce offspring (6)
People ordained for religious service (6)
Pleasing and wholesome in appearance (6)
Public officer who investigates deaths (7)
Rapid shaking (9)
Shacks (8)
Strange; odd (5)
Strong in body (5)
The forward, discharging end of the barrel of a firearm (6)
Things that are undesirable or troublesome (8)
To Awaken (5)
To get along (4)
To jab or poke with a pointed object (4)
To keep off (4)
To solve problems in arithmetic (6)
To worry (4)
With a leg on each side (7)
Moves or acts swiftly (7)

Day No Pigs Would Die Vocabulary Word Search 2 Answer Key

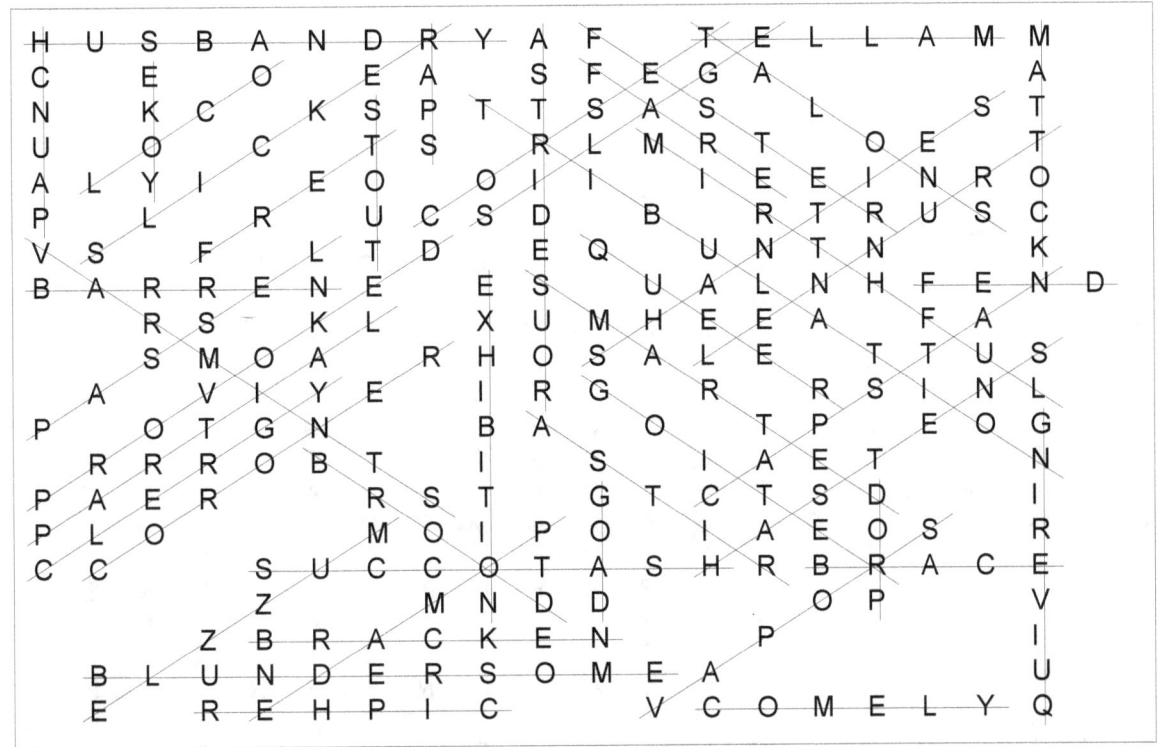

Breeding livestock (9)
A crossbar with two U-shaped pieces (4)
A digging tool with a flat blade (7)
A large quantity or group (6)
A long stick with a pointed end (4)
A pair of like things (5)
A perfumed hair ointment (6)
A plastic or rubber raincoat (7)
A potbelly (6)
A public showing (10)
A short-handled hammer with a large head (6)
A stew of corn, lima beans, and tomatoes (9)
A weedy fern (7)
A wooden peg that swells when wet (7)
An apparatus used for hoisting weights (7)
An enlargement of the thyroid gland (6)
An undergarment that supports the waist and hips (6)
Caused a stinging pain (7)
Causing mistakes (11)
Claws of a bird of prey (6)
Distress; suffering (11)
Fermented green plants (6)
Full of gladness and gaiety (8)
Having a liking or fondness for (7)
Incited to anger or resentment (8)

Irritate (6)
Kept for producing young (5)
Low spirits (6)
Mad; insane (4)
Moving about (5)
Non-metallic light-colored mineral (4)
Not able to produce offspring (6)
People ordained for religious service (6)
Pleasing and wholesome in appearance (6)
Public officer who investigates deaths (7)
Rapid shaking (9)
Shacks (8)
Strange; odd (5)
Strong in body (5)
The forward, discharging end of the barrel of a firearm (6)
Things that are undesirable or troublesome (8)
To Awaken (5)
To get along (4)
To jab or poke with a pointed object (4)
To keep off (4)
To solve problems in arithmetic (6)
To worry (4)
With a leg on each side (7)
Moves or acts swiftly (7)

Day No Pigs Would Die Vocabulary Word Search 3

```
C L E R G Y T D M I R T H F U L H R M M
F S Q G C D E R C A V T N H G A X U O U
V T C F H K C M U V T N F I K Y S Z Z T
H N R D O S S A G N Q T T D Q J B Z Z B
F I F V M U M W P R S R O Q T L A E L K
D M O T C C A M Q S A E D C E P N D T J
C R D Q X C R T C P T D L S K J D I R K
P A M J P O T L N O B A S C Q G R R R F
J V H A S T E N S Y R A N O S H Y T I S
P D J J F A D M K E P O F R S Q P S B M
M R K J K S Y Z T N C N S S Y C A U D S
D R O M V H G I T B W Q C E P R T S L H
W S V S R D O V N L C R U T R D B K A A
W J F M P G Z N Q U B X C I V P S T I N
P Z B D A E W S S N R Q O T V A P B O T
V O X Y Y L R K D D A D M Z W E P F N I
S T M F C D L O R E C N E G F S R O E E
B V A A G R O E U R K E L J O P P I R S
G R D M D R R E T S E F Y N T A L O N G
E W A D B E P U I O N C E O U R D K L G
F Q O C L T O L K M A R I N K R R I O F
D R M N E T A B Q E R S C P E E C V B W
P Y E R S G S H M A N H T E H K C C B H
L J Y T E G R X B S G X U I E E O S J G
E X H I B I T I O N V Q B R L R B G G
```

ASTIR	COMELY	HASTENS	POMADE	SMARTED
ASTRIDE	CORONER	HUSBANDRY	PROD	SPAR
BARREN	CORSET	LOCO	PROSPEROUS	STOUT
BLUNDERSOME	EXHIBITION	MALLET	PROVOKED	SUCCOTASH
BRACE	FARE	MATTOCK	QUEER	TALONS
BRACKEN	FEND	MIRTHFUL	QUIVERING	TRIBULATION
BROOD	FESTER	MUZZLE	ROUSE	TRUNNEL
CAPSTAN	FRET	PARTIAL	SHANTIES	VAPORS
CIPHER	GOAD	PASSEL	SILAGE	VARMINTS
CLERGY	GOITER	PAUNCH	SLICKER	YOKE

Day No Pigs Would Die Vocabulary Word Search 3 Answer Key

ASTIR	COMELY	HASTENS	POMADE	SMARTED
ASTRIDE	CORONER	HUSBANDRY	PROD	SPAR
BARREN	CORSET	LOCO	PROSPEROUS	STOUT
BLUNDERSOME	EXHIBITION	MALLET	PROVOKED	SUCCOTASH
BRACE	FARE	MATTOCK	QUEER	TALONS
BRACKEN	FEND	MIRTHFUL	QUIVERING	TRIBULATION
BROOD	FESTER	MUZZLE	ROUSE	TRUNNEL
CAPSTAN	FRET	PARTIAL	SHANTIES	VAPORS
CIPHER	GOAD	PASSEL	SILAGE	VARMINTS
CLERGY	GOITER	PAUNCH	SLICKER	YOKE

Day No Pigs Would Die Vocabulary Word Search 4

ASTIR	COMELY	HASTENS	POMADE	SMARTED
ASTRIDE	CORONER	HUSBANDRY	PROD	SPAR
BARREN	CORSET	LOCO	PROSPEROUS	STOUT
BLUNDERSOME	EXHIBITION	MALLET	PROVOKED	SUCCOTASH
BRACE	FARE	MATTOCK	QUEER	TALONS
BRACKEN	FEND	MIRTHFUL	QUIVERING	TRIBULATION
BROOD	FESTER	MUZZLE	ROUSE	TRUNNEL
CAPSTAN	FRET	PARTIAL	SHANTIES	VAPORS
CIPHER	GOAD	PASSEL	SILAGE	VARMINTS
CLERGY	GOITER	PAUNCH	SLICKER	YOKE

Day No Pigs Would Die Vocabulary Word Search 4 Answer Key

ASTIR	COMELY	HASTENS	POMADE	SMARTED
ASTRIDE	CORONER	HUSBANDRY	PROD	SPAR
BARREN	CORSET	LOCO	PROSPEROUS	STOUT
BLUNDERSOME	EXHIBITION	MALLET	PROVOKED	SUCCOTASH
BRACE	FARE	MATTOCK	QUEER	TALONS
BRACKEN	FEND	MIRTHFUL	QUIVERING	TRIBULATION
BROOD	FESTER	MUZZLE	ROUSE	TRUNNEL
CAPSTAN	FRET	PARTIAL	SHANTIES	VAPORS
CIPHER	GOAD	PASSEL	SILAGE	VARMINTS
CLERGY	GOITER	PAUNCH	SLICKER	YOKE

Day No Pigs Would Die Vocabulary Crossword 1

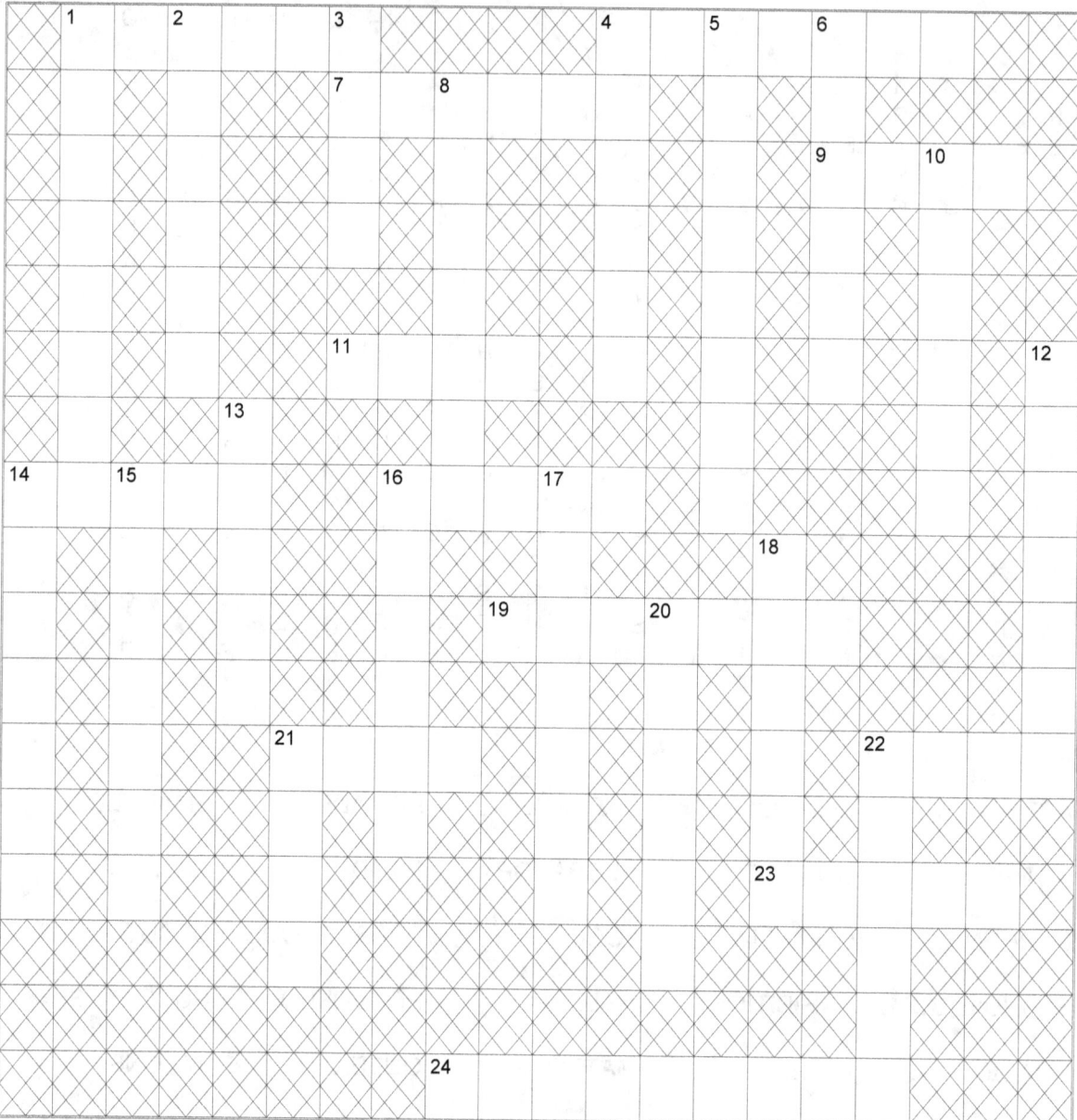

Across
1. Low spirits
4. An apparatus used for hoisting weights
7. A large quantity or group
9. Mad; insane
11. A crossbar with two U-shaped pieces
14. Moving about
16. A pair of like things
19. A weedy fern
21. To worry
22. To jab or poke with a pointed object
23. To Awaken
24. A stew of corn, lima beans, and tomatoes

Down
1. Things that are undesirable or troublesome
2. A perfumed hair ointment
3. Non-metallic light-colored mineral
4. People ordained for religious service
5. Incited to anger or resentment
6. Claws of a bird of prey
8. A plastic or rubber raincoat
10. Pleasing and wholesome in appearance
12. Caused a stinging pain
13. Kept for producing young
14. With a leg on each side
15. A wooden peg that swells when wet
16. Not able to produce offspring
17. Public officer who investigates deaths
18. Irritate
20. To solve problems in arithmetic
21. To keep off
22. A potbelly

Day No Pigs Would Die Vocabulary Crossword 1 Answer Key

	1 V	2 A	P	3 S	O	R	S		4 C	5 A	P	6 S	T	A	N	
	A	O		7 P	8 A	S	S	E	L	R		A				
	R	M		A					E	O		9 L	O	10 C	O	
	M	A		R					R	V		O		O		
	I	D		I					G	O		N		M		
	N	E		11 Y	O	K	E		Y	K		S		E		12 S
	T		13 B				E			E				L		M
14 A	S	15 T	I	R		16 B	R	A	17 C	E		D			Y	A
S		R	O			A			O			18 F				R
T		U	O			R		19 B	R	A	20 C	K	E	N		T
R		N	D			R			O		I		S			E
I		N		21 F	R	E	T		N		P		T		22 P	R	O	D
D		E		E			N		E		H		E		A		
E		L		N					R		E		23 R	O	U	S	E
				D							R				N		
						24 S	U	C	C	O	T	A	S	H		

Across
1. Low spirits
4. An apparatus used for hoisting weights
7. A large quantity or group
9. Mad; insane
11. A crossbar with two U-shaped pieces
14. Moving about
16. A pair of like things
19. A weedy fern
21. To worry
22. To jab or poke with a pointed object
23. To Awaken
24. A stew of corn, lima beans, and tomatoes

Down
1. Things that are undesirable or troublesome
2. A perfumed hair ointment
3. Non-metallic light-colored mineral
4. People ordained for religious service
5. Incited to anger or resentment
6. Claws of a bird of prey
8. A plastic or rubber raincoat
10. Pleasing and wholesome in appearance
12. Caused a stinging pain
13. Kept for producing young
14. With a leg on each side
15. A wooden peg that swells when wet
16. Not able to produce offspring
17. Public officer who investigates deaths
18. Irritate
20. To solve problems in arithmetic
21. To keep off
22. A potbelly

Day No Pigs Would Die Vocabulary Crossword 2

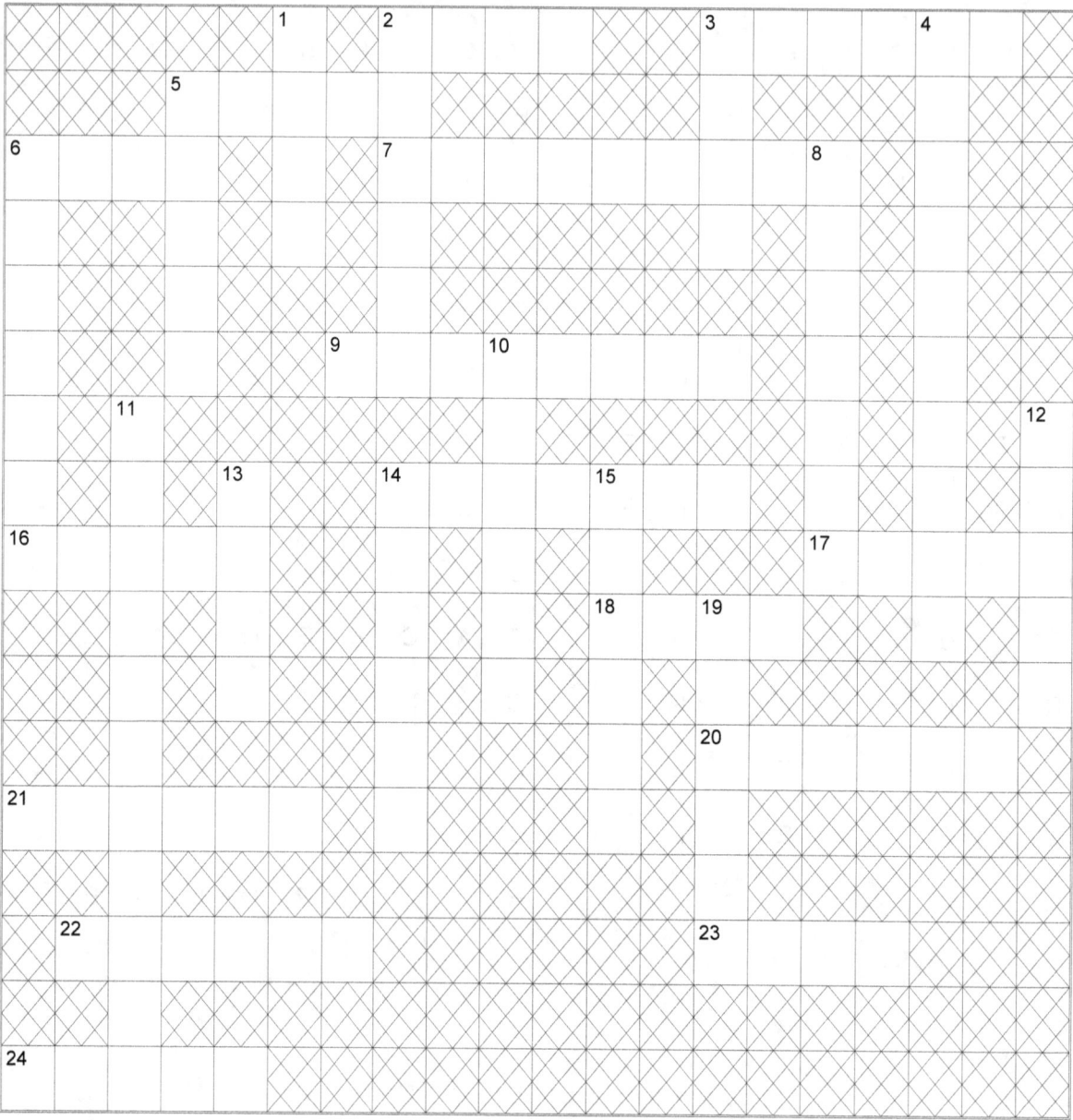

Across
2. To worry
3. An enlargement of the thyroid gland
5. A pair of like things
6. Non-metallic light-colored mineral
7. A stew of corn, lima beans, and tomatoes
9. Incited to anger or resentment
14. An apparatus used for hoisting weights
16. To Awaken
17. Strong in body
18. Mad; insane
20. The forward, discharging end of the barrel of a firearm
21. Not able to produce offspring
22. A perfumed hair ointment
23. A crossbar with two U-shaped pieces
24. Strange; odd

Down
1. To get along
2. Irritate
3. A long stick with a pointed end
4. A public showing
5. Kept for producing young
6. A plastic or rubber raincoat
8. Moves or acts swiftly
10. Low spirits
11. Causing mistakes
12. Moving about
13. To keep off
14. People ordained for religious service
15. Claws of a bird of prey
19. Pleasing and wholesome in appearance

Day No Pigs Would Die Vocabulary Crossword 2 Answer Key

Across
- 2. To worry
- 3. An enlargement of the thyroid gland
- 5. A pair of like things
- 6. Non-metallic light-colored mineral
- 7. A stew of corn, lima beans, and tomatoes
- 9. Incited to anger or resentment
- 14. An apparatus used for hoisting weights
- 16. To Awaken
- 17. Strong in body
- 18. Mad; insane
- 20. The forward, discharging end of the barrel of a firearm
- 21. Not able to produce offspring
- 22. A perfumed hair ointment
- 23. A crossbar with two U-shaped pieces
- 24. Strange; odd

Down
- 1. To get along
- 2. Irritate
- 3. A long stick with a pointed end
- 4. A public showing
- 5. Kept for producing young
- 6. A plastic or rubber raincoat
- 8. Moves or acts swiftly
- 10. Low spirits
- 11. Causing mistakes
- 12. Moving about
- 13. To keep off
- 14. People ordained for religious service
- 15. Claws of a bird of prey
- 19. Pleasing and wholesome in appearance

Day No Pigs Would Die Vocabulary Crossword 3

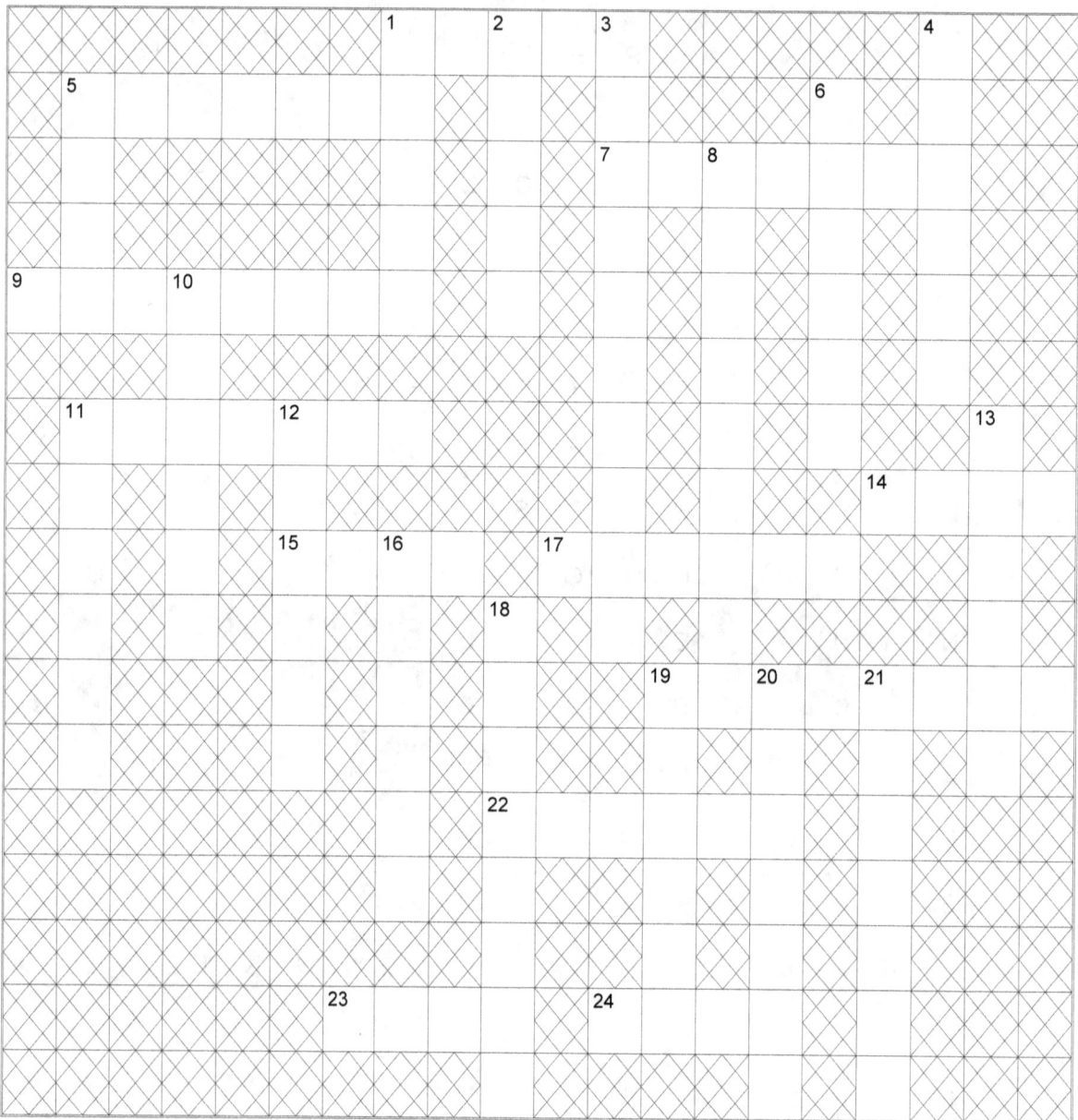

Across
1. A pair of like things
5. A plastic or rubber raincoat
7. Moves or acts swiftly
9. Incited to anger or resentment
11. An apparatus used for hoisting weights
14. A long stick with a pointed end
15. Mad; insane
17. A perfumed hair ointment
19. Shacks
22. A short-handled hammer with a large head
23. To worry
24. To keep off

Down
1. Kept for producing young
2. Moving about
3. A public showing
4. A large quantity or group
5. Non-metallic light-colored mineral
6. Irritate
8. A stew of corn, lima beans, and tomatoes
10. Low spirits
11. People ordained for religious service
12. Claws of a bird of prey
13. Not able to produce offspring
16. Pleasing and wholesome in appearance
18. Things that are undesirable or troublesome
19. Fermented green plants
20. With a leg on each side
21. A wooden peg that swells when wet

Day No Pigs Would Die Vocabulary Crossword 3 Answer Key

					¹B	²R	³A	C	⁴E				⁴P	
⁵S	L	I	C	K	E	R		S		X		⁶F		A
	P				O		T		⁷H	⁸A	S	T	E	N	S
	A				O		I		I		U		S		S
⁹P	R	O	¹⁰V	O	K	E	D		R		B		⁸C		T	E		L
			A								I		C		E		L
¹¹C	A	P	S	¹²T	A	N					T		O		R	¹³B
	L			O		A					I		T		¹⁴G	O	A	D
	E			R		¹⁵L	O	¹⁶C	O		¹⁷P	O	M	A	D	E		R
	R			S		O		O		¹⁸V		N		S				R
	G					O		M		A			¹⁹S	H	²⁰A	N	²¹T	I	E	S
	Y					S		E		R			I		S		R		N
								L		²²M	A	L	L	E	T		U		
								Y		I			A		R		N		
										N			G		I		N		
						²³F	R	E	T			²⁴F	E	N	D		E		
									S						E		L		

Across
1. A pair of like things
3. A public showing
4. A large quantity or group
5. A plastic or rubber raincoat
5. Non-metallic light-colored mineral
6. Irritate
7. Moves or acts swiftly
8. A stew of corn, lima beans, and tomatoes
9. Incited to anger or resentment
10. Low spirits
11. An apparatus used for hoisting weights
11. People ordained for religious service
12. Claws of a bird of prey
13. Not able to produce offspring
14. A long stick with a pointed end
15. Mad; insane
16. Pleasing and wholesome in appearance
17. A perfumed hair ointment
18. Things that are undesirable or troublesome
19. Shacks
19. Fermented green plants
20. With a leg on each side
21. A wooden peg that swells when wet
22. A short-handled hammer with a large head
23. To worry
24. To keep off

Down
1. Kept for producing young
2. Moving about

Day No Pigs Would Die Vocabulary Crossword 4

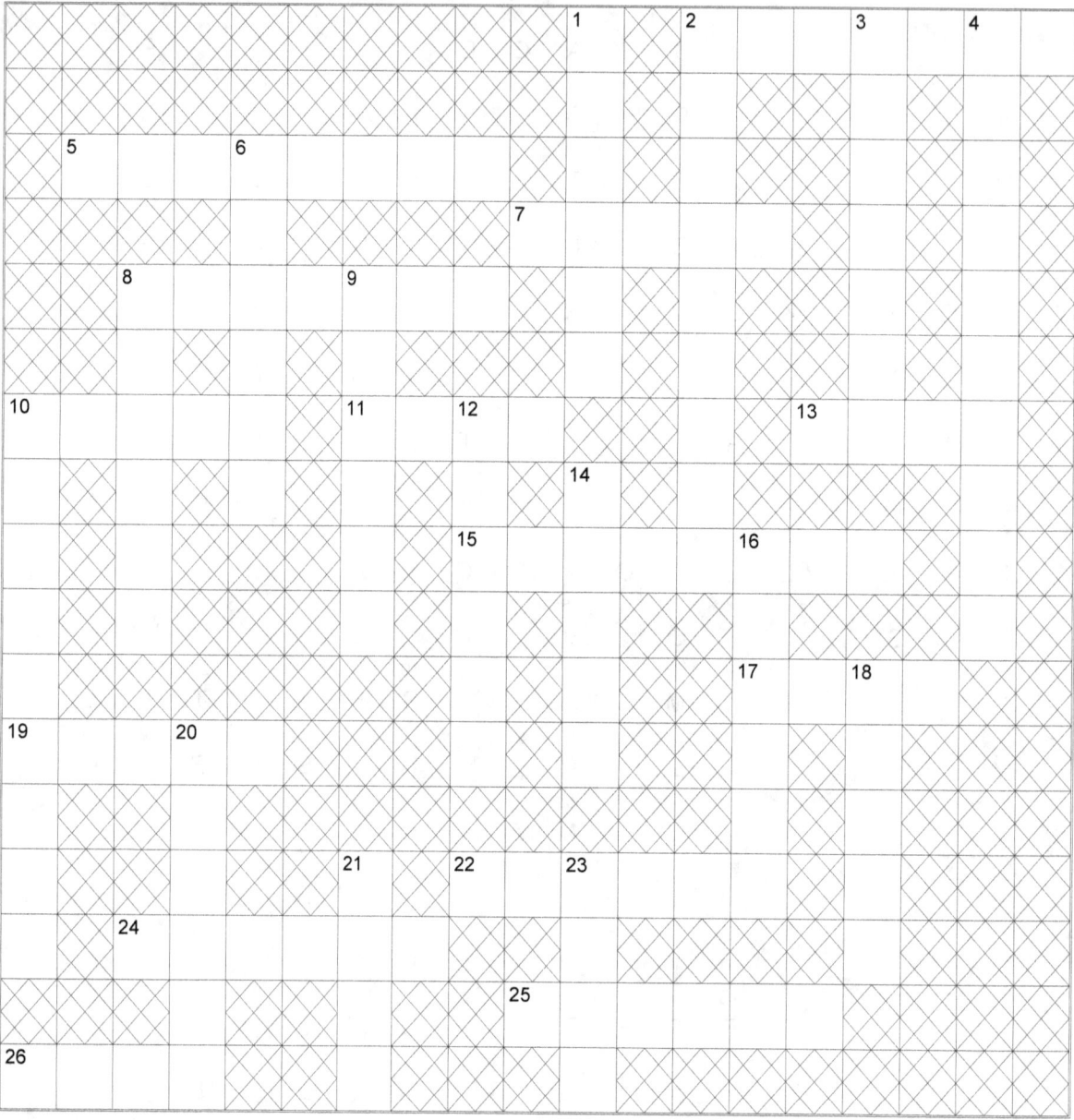

Across
2. A plastic or rubber raincoat
5. Incited to anger or resentment
7. A pair of like things
8. An apparatus used for hoisting weights
10. Strange; odd
11. Mad; insane
13. To worry
15. Full of gladness and gaiety
17. Non-metallic light-colored mineral
19. To Awaken
22. To solve problems in arithmetic
24. A large quantity or group
25. A perfumed hair ointment
26. A crossbar with two U-shaped pieces

Down
1. Not able to produce offspring
2. A stew of corn, lima beans, and tomatoes
3. Public officer who investigates deaths
4. A public showing
6. Low spirits
8. People ordained for religious service
9. Claws of a bird of prey
10. Rapid shaking
12. Pleasing and wholesome in appearance
14. Kept for producing young
16. Irritate
18. Moving about
20. Fermented green plants
21. To keep off
23. To jab or poke with a pointed object

Day No Pigs Would Die Vocabulary Crossword 4 Answer Key

							1 B		2 S	L	I	3 C	K	4 E	R
							A		U			O		X	
		5 P	R	O	6 V	O	K	E	D			R		H	
					A			7 B	R	A	C	E		I	
			8 C	A	P	9 S	T	A	N			O		B	
			L		O	A		E				E		I	
10 Q	U	E	E	R		11 L	O	12 C	O		13 F	R	E	T	
U			R			O		O		14 B		S		I	
I			G			N		15 M	I	R	T	H	16 F	U	L
V			Y			S		E		O			E		O	N
E								L		O		17 S	P	18 A	R
19 R	O	20 U	S	E				Y		D		T		S	
I		I										E		T	
N		L			21 F		22 C	I	23 P	H	E	R		I	
G		24 P	A	S	S	E	L		R					R	
		G			N			25 P	O	M	A	D	E	
26 Y	O	K	E		D				D					

Across
- 2. A plastic or rubber raincoat
- 5. Incited to anger or resentment
- 7. A pair of like things
- 8. An apparatus used for hoisting weights
- 10. Strange; odd
- 11. Mad; insane
- 13. To worry
- 15. Full of gladness and gaiety
- 17. Non-metallic light-colored mineral
- 19. To Awaken
- 22. To solve problems in arithmetic
- 24. A large quantity or group
- 25. A perfumed hair ointment
- 26. A crossbar with two U-shaped pieces

Down
- 1. Not able to produce offspring
- 2. A stew of corn, lima beans, and tomatoes
- 3. Public officer who investigates deaths
- 4. A public showing
- 6. Low spirits
- 8. People ordained for religious service
- 9. Claws of a bird of prey
- 10. Rapid shaking
- 12. Pleasing and wholesome in appearance
- 14. Kept for producing young
- 16. Irritate
- 18. Moving about
- 20. Fermented green plants
- 21. To keep off
- 23. To jab or poke with a pointed object

Day No Pigs Would Die Vocabulary Juggle Letters 1

1. TANHSES = 1. _____
   Moves or acts swiftly

2. TRFE = 2. _____
   To worry

3. RODP = 3. _____
   To jab or poke with a pointed object

4. DGAO = 4. _____
   A long stick with a pointed end

5. IOBATLRUNIT = 5. _____
   Distress; suffering

6. EOLCMY = 6. _____
   Pleasing and wholesome in appearance

7. NDFE = 7. _____
   To keep off

8. CUHTOSASC = 8. _____
   A stew of corn, lima beans, and tomatoes

9. DERPOKOV = 9. _____
   Incited to anger or resentment

10. REETFS =10. _____
    Irritate

11. XBOTINIEIH =11. _____
    A public showing

12. ISTRA =12. _____
    Moving about

13. AFER =13. _____
    To get along

14. GISEAL =14. _____
    Fermented green plants

15. UERSO =15. _____
    To Awaken

Day No Pigs Would Die Vocabulary Juggle Letters 1 Answer Key

1. TANHSES = 1. HASTENS
Moves or acts swiftly

2. TRFE = 2. FRET
To worry

3. RODP = 3. PROD
To jab or poke with a pointed object

4. DGAO = 4. GOAD
A long stick with a pointed end

5. IOBATLRUNIT = 5. TRIBULATION
Distress; suffering

6. EOLCMY = 6. COMELY
Pleasing and wholesome in appearance

7. NDFE = 7. FEND
To keep off

8. CUHTOSASC = 8. SUCCOTASH
A stew of corn, lima beans, and tomatoes

9. DERPOKOV = 9. PROVOKED
Incited to anger or resentment

10. REETFS = 10. FESTER
Irritate

11. XBOTINIEIH = 11. EXHIBITION
A public showing

12. ISTRA = 12. ASTIR
Moving about

13. AFER = 13. FARE
To get along

14. GISEAL = 14. SILAGE
Fermented green plants

15. UERSO = 15. ROUSE
To Awaken

Day No Pigs Would Die Vocabulary Juggle Letters 2

1. ANCTAPS = 1. _____
   An apparatus used for hoisting weights

2. RSATI = 2. _____
   Moving about

3. ODPR = 3. _____
   To jab or poke with a pointed object

4. RCERNOO = 4. _____
   Public officer who investigates deaths

5. ERFT = 5. _____
   To worry

6. COOL = 6. _____
   Mad; insane

7. CPNAUH = 7. _____
   A potbelly

8. AKOCTMT = 8. _____
   A digging tool with a flat blade

9. MARETSD = 9. _____
   Caused a stinging pain

10. SRRSUPOPOE =10. _____
    Successful

11. LSIGEA =11. _____
    Fermented green plants

12. EMLTLA =12. _____
    A short-handled hammer with a large head

13. KEOY =13. _____
    A crossbar with two U-shaped pieces

14. MDAPEO =14. _____
    A perfumed hair ointment

15. NEIGRIUVQ =15. _____
    Rapid shaking

Day No Pigs Would Die Vocabulary Juggle Letters 2 Answer Key

1. ANCTAPS = 1. CAPSTAN
An apparatus used for hoisting weights

2. RSATI = 2. ASTIR
Moving about

3. ODPR = 3. PROD
To jab or poke with a pointed object

4. RCERNOO = 4. CORONER
Public officer who investigates deaths

5. ERFT = 5. FRET
To worry

6. COOL = 6. LOCO
Mad; insane

7. CPNAUH = 7. PAUNCH
A potbelly

8. AKOCTMT = 8. MATTOCK
A digging tool with a flat blade

9. MARETSD = 9. SMARTED
Caused a stinging pain

10. SRRSUPOPOE = 10. PROSPEROUS
Successful

11. LSIGEA = 11. SILAGE
Fermented green plants

12. EMLTLA = 12. MALLET
A short-handled hammer with a large head

13. KEOY = 13. YOKE
A crossbar with two U-shaped pieces

14. MDAPEO = 14. POMADE
A perfumed hair ointment

15. NEIGRIUVQ = 15. QUIVERING
Rapid shaking

Day No Pigs Would Die Vocabulary Juggle Letters 3

1. NLTNEUR = 1. _____
A wooden peg that swells when wet

2. OLOC = 2. _____
Mad; insane

3. PDRO = 3. _____
To jab or poke with a pointed object

4. USORLBEMNDE = 4. _____
Causing mistakes

5. LEUMZZ = 5. _____
The forward, discharging end of the barrel of a firearm

6. ELTLMA = 6. _____
A short-handled hammer with a large head

7. ESOTRC = 7. _____
An undergarment that supports the waist and hips

8. TSEFER = 8. _____
Irritate

9. RCBKNAE = 9. _____
A weedy fern

10. SEAHTSN = 10. _____
Moves or acts swiftly

11. OTSTU = 11. _____
Strong in body

12. RKOODEVP = 12. _____
Incited to anger or resentment

13. TFMULIHR = 13. _____
Full of gladness and gaiety

14. OPORESPUSR = 14. _____
Successful

15. OGAD = 15. _____
A long stick with a pointed end

Day No Pigs Would Die Vocabulary Juggle Letters 3 Answer Key

1. NLTNEUR = 1. TRUNNEL
   A wooden peg that swells when wet

2. OLOC = 2. LOCO
   Mad; insane

3. PDRO = 3. PROD
   To jab or poke with a pointed object

4. USORLBEMNDE = 4. BLUNDERSOME
   Causing mistakes

5. LEUMZZ = 5. MUZZLE
   The forward, discharging end of the barrel of a firearm

6. ELTLMA = 6. MALLET
   A short-handled hammer with a large head

7. ESOTRC = 7. CORSET
   An undergarment that supports the waist and hips

8. TSEFER = 8. FESTER
   Irritate

9. RCBKNAE = 9. BRACKEN
   A weedy fern

10. SEAHTSN =10. HASTENS
    Moves or acts swiftly

11. OTSTU =11. STOUT
    Strong in body

12. RKOODEVP =12. PROVOKED
    Incited to anger or resentment

13. TFMULIHR =13. MIRTHFUL
    Full of gladness and gaiety

14. OPORESPUSR =14. PROSPEROUS
    Successful

15. OGAD =15. GOAD
    A long stick with a pointed end

Day No Pigs Would Die Vocabulary Juggle Letters 4

1. IOXTIBHEIN = 1. _____
   A public showing

2. COLO = 2. _____
   Mad; insane

3. OPRAVS = 3. _____
   Low spirits

4. PSAR = 4. _____
   Non-metallic light-colored mineral

5. STRIA = 5. _____
   Moving about

6. TOTUS = 6. _____
   Strong in body

7. MRDTSEA = 7. _____
   Caused a stinging pain

8. NAUPCH = 8. _____
   A potbelly

9. EKCBNAR = 9. _____
   A weedy fern

10. RBOOD = 10. _____
    Kept for producing young

11. ESPRPUROSO = 11. _____
    Successful

12. YERGLC = 12. _____
    People ordained for religious service

13. RTOCSE = 13. _____
    An undergarment that supports the waist and hips

14. EORTGI = 14. _____
    An enlargement of the thyroid gland

15. DENF = 15. _____
    To keep off

Day No Pigs Would Die Vocabulary Juggle Letters 4 Answer Key

1. IOXTIBHEIN = 1. EXHIBITION
   A public showing

2. COLO = 2. LOCO
   Mad; insane

3. OPRAVS = 3. VAPORS
   Low spirits

4. PSAR = 4. SPAR
   Non-metallic light-colored mineral

5. STRIA = 5. ASTIR
   Moving about

6. TOTUS = 6. STOUT
   Strong in body

7. MRDTSEA = 7. SMARTED
   Caused a stinging pain

8. NAUPCH = 8. PAUNCH
   A potbelly

9. EKCBNAR = 9. BRACKEN
   A weedy fern

10. RBOOD = 10. BROOD
    Kept for producing young

11. ESPRPUROSO = 11. PROSPEROUS
    Successful

12. YERGLC = 12. CLERGY
    People ordained for religious service

13. RTOCSE = 13. CORSET
    An undergarment that supports the waist and hips

14. EORTGI = 14. GOITER
    An enlargement of the thyroid gland

15. DENF = 15. FEND
    To keep off

ASTIR	Moving about
ASTRIDE	With a leg on each side
BARREN	Not able to produce offspring
BLUNDERSOME	Causing mistakes
BRACE	A pair of like things
BRACKEN	A weedy fern

BROOD	Kept for producing young
CAPSTAN	An apparatus used for hoisting weights
CIPHER	To solve problems in arithmetic
CLERGY	People ordained for religious service
COMELY	Pleasing and wholesome in appearance
CORONER	Public officer who investigates deaths

CORSET	An undergarment that supports the waist and hips
EXHIBITION	A public showing
FARE	To get along
FEND	To keep off
FESTER	Irritate
FRET	To worry

GOAD	A long stick with a pointed end
GOITER	An enlargement of the thyroid gland
HASTENS	Moves or acts swiftly
HUSBANDRY	Breeding livestock
LOCO	Mad; insane
MALLET	A short-handled hammer with a large head

MATTOCK	A digging tool with a flat blade
MIRTHFUL	Full of gladness and gaiety
MUZZLE	The forward, discharging end of the barrel of a firearm
PARTIAL	Having a liking or fondness for
PASSEL	A large quantity or group
PAUNCH	A potbelly

POMADE	A perfumed hair ointment
PROD	To jab or poke with a pointed object
PROSPEROUS	Successful
PROVOKED	Incited to anger or resentment
QUEER	Strange; odd
QUIVERING	Rapid shaking

ROUSE	To Awaken
SHANTIES	Shacks
SILAGE	Fermented green plants
SLICKER	A plastic or rubber raincoat
SMARTED	Caused a stinging pain
SPAR	Non-metallic light-colored mineral

STOUT	Strong in body
SUCCOTASH	A stew of corn, lima beans, and tomatoes
TALONS	Claws of a bird of prey
TRIBULATION	Distress; suffering
TRUNNEL	A wooden peg that swells when wet
VAPORS	Low spirits

VARMINTS	Things that are undesirable or troublesome
YOKE	A crossbar with two U-shaped pieces

Day No Pigs Would Die Vocabulary

BARREN	YOKE	COMELY	QUEER	LOCO
SILAGE	EXHIBITION	BRACE	TALONS	GOITER
HASTENS	CAPSTAN	FREE SPACE	ASTRIDE	PROD
PROSPEROUS	MATTOCK	QUIVERING	POMADE	VARMINTS
GOAD	HUSBANDRY	FARE	PROVOKED	PASSEL

Day No Pigs Would Die Vocabulary

FRET	MIRTHFUL	BLUNDERSOME	BRACKEN	FEND
SLICKER	MALLET	SUCCOTASH	FESTER	SMARTED
CLERGY	PAUNCH	FREE SPACE	SHANTIES	ROUSE
PARTIAL	STOUT	CIPHER	BROOD	SPAR
TRIBULATION	CORSET	MUZZLE	CORONER	TRUNNEL

Day No Pigs Would Die Vocabulary

QUIVERING	CORSET	LOCO	PROVOKED	TRIBULATION
FEND	HUSBANDRY	ASTRIDE	COMELY	GOITER
GOAD	FRET	FREE SPACE	SILAGE	CIPHER
QUEER	STOUT	SPAR	BLUNDERSOME	BARREN
FESTER	TRUNNEL	CAPSTAN	SMARTED	POMADE

Day No Pigs Would Die Vocabulary

YOKE	MATTOCK	ASTIR	SHANTIES	SLICKER
CORONER	PROD	PAUNCH	TALONS	MIRTHFUL
BRACE	PROSPEROUS	FREE SPACE	HASTENS	MALLET
CLERGY	SUCCOTASH	VAPORS	EXHIBITION	BROOD
FARE	ROUSE	PARTIAL	VARMINTS	BRACKEN

Day No Pigs Would Die Vocabulary

VARMINTS	SHANTIES	QUEER	CIPHER	GOITER
BRACKEN	PROSPEROUS	ASTRIDE	PASSEL	CORONER
FARE	SLICKER	FREE SPACE	BARREN	SILAGE
ROUSE	TRIBULATION	MALLET	BRACE	MATTOCK
VAPORS	FEND	CLERGY	SPAR	BLUNDERSOME

Day No Pigs Would Die Vocabulary

PROVOKED	ASTIR	SUCCOTASH	LOCO	PARTIAL
EXHIBITION	COMELY	GOAD	CAPSTAN	SMARTED
PROD	FESTER	FREE SPACE	STOUT	CORSET
HASTENS	TRUNNEL	QUIVERING	HUSBANDRY	PAUNCH
BROOD	MUZZLE	TALONS	POMADE	FRET

Day No Pigs Would Die Vocabulary

POMADE	QUEER	CORSET	HASTENS	PASSEL
TALONS	BRACE	COMELY	GOITER	MUZZLE
MIRTHFUL	SLICKER	FREE SPACE	QUIVERING	PAUNCH
FESTER	TRIBULATION	CLERGY	MATTOCK	BARREN
PROVOKED	MALLET	BLUNDERSOME	CORONER	SPAR

Day No Pigs Would Die Vocabulary

PARTIAL	PROD	SHANTIES	VAPORS	SMARTED
FARE	ROUSE	GOAD	ASTIR	ASTRIDE
PROSPEROUS	CIPHER	FREE SPACE	BRACKEN	FRET
CAPSTAN	SUCCOTASH	YOKE	FEND	TRUNNEL
LOCO	EXHIBITION	SILAGE	HUSBANDRY	VARMINTS

Day No Pigs Would Die Vocabulary

TRIBULATION	BROOD	SHANTIES	PARTIAL	HASTENS
SLICKER	FEND	FESTER	PROSPEROUS	CLERGY
SILAGE	TALONS	FREE SPACE	GOITER	HUSBANDRY
SMARTED	STOUT	VARMINTS	FARE	ASTRIDE
LOCO	CAPSTAN	CORONER	PROVOKED	YOKE

Day No Pigs Would Die Vocabulary

PAUNCH	GOAD	BRACE	BLUNDERSOME	SPAR
QUEER	VAPORS	ROUSE	CIPHER	ASTIR
FRET	POMADE	FREE SPACE	CORSET	PROD
QUIVERING	BRACKEN	MIRTHFUL	TRUNNEL	MALLET
BARREN	MATTOCK	MUZZLE	PASSEL	COMELY

Day No Pigs Would Die Vocabulary

MIRTHFUL	COMELY	BLUNDERSOME	MATTOCK	STOUT
BARREN	TALONS	CIPHER	TRUNNEL	HUSBANDRY
TRIBULATION	LOCO	FREE SPACE	FARE	FESTER
CLERGY	SPAR	SLICKER	SMARTED	FEND
QUIVERING	SHANTIES	POMADE	BROOD	FRET

Day No Pigs Would Die Vocabulary

SILAGE	YOKE	PASSEL	VARMINTS	ASTIR
MALLET	VAPORS	PROSPEROUS	PROD	PAUNCH
CORONER	BRACE	FREE SPACE	GOAD	CORSET
PARTIAL	SUCCOTASH	ROUSE	EXHIBITION	HASTENS
CAPSTAN	BRACKEN	MUZZLE	PROVOKED	QUEER

Day No Pigs Would Die Vocabulary

CORSET	BRACKEN	BROOD	FRET	ASTIR
PROD	SILAGE	FESTER	SHANTIES	COMELY
HASTENS	POMADE	FREE SPACE	SMARTED	EXHIBITION
PARTIAL	MUZZLE	TRIBULATION	FARE	QUEER
CLERGY	PROVOKED	SLICKER	SUCCOTASH	BRACE

Day No Pigs Would Die Vocabulary

HUSBANDRY	YOKE	QUIVERING	CIPHER	MATTOCK
CORONER	STOUT	TRUNNEL	TALONS	GOITER
FEND	MALLET	FREE SPACE	CAPSTAN	PAUNCH
ROUSE	BLUNDERSOME	VARMINTS	SPAR	ASTRIDE
PASSEL	BARREN	PROSPEROUS	VAPORS	GOAD

Day No Pigs Would Die Vocabulary

SHANTIES	BRACE	PROD	CAPSTAN	FRET
PARTIAL	BARREN	FARE	BLUNDERSOME	FEND
TRIBULATION	MATTOCK	FREE SPACE	GOAD	COMELY
ROUSE	HUSBANDRY	HASTENS	CORSET	MIRTHFUL
ASTRIDE	ASTIR	STOUT	CLERGY	LOCO

Day No Pigs Would Die Vocabulary

CIPHER	POMADE	PAUNCH	SILAGE	PROSPEROUS
CORONER	SPAR	PASSEL	SLICKER	MALLET
SMARTED	BROOD	FREE SPACE	MUZZLE	BRACKEN
QUEER	GOITER	SUCCOTASH	VAPORS	FESTER
PROVOKED	TRUNNEL	TALONS	YOKE	EXHIBITION

Day No Pigs Would Die Vocabulary

TRIBULATION	QUIVERING	VAPORS	YOKE	BRACKEN
HASTENS	PAUNCH	TALONS	FRET	EXHIBITION
CORSET	SUCCOTASH	FREE SPACE	CLERGY	VARMINTS
GOAD	MUZZLE	SPAR	FARE	PROVOKED
ROUSE	CAPSTAN	PROD	PARTIAL	BROOD

Day No Pigs Would Die Vocabulary

GOITER	PASSEL	SHANTIES	FEND	SLICKER
SMARTED	STOUT	SILAGE	MALLET	QUEER
MIRTHFUL	POMADE	FREE SPACE	HUSBANDRY	FESTER
CORONER	BLUNDERSOME	ASTIR	TRUNNEL	BRACE
MATTOCK	BARREN	COMELY	PROSPEROUS	ASTRIDE

Day No Pigs Would Die Vocabulary

SLICKER	ASTIR	BARREN	COMELY	ASTRIDE
FESTER	SUCCOTASH	POMADE	STOUT	SILAGE
SPAR	QUEER	FREE SPACE	PROD	LOCO
PROSPEROUS	TRIBULATION	PAUNCH	MUZZLE	GOITER
MALLET	SMARTED	TALONS	QUIVERING	CORONER

Day No Pigs Would Die Vocabulary

EXHIBITION	HUSBANDRY	FEND	FRET	TRUNNEL
VAPORS	BLUNDERSOME	ROUSE	HASTENS	YOKE
PARTIAL	CIPHER	FREE SPACE	BRACKEN	MATTOCK
CORSET	FARE	SHANTIES	BRACE	PASSEL
MIRTHFUL	CAPSTAN	GOAD	BROOD	VARMINTS

Day No Pigs Would Die Vocabulary

POMADE	MUZZLE	PASSEL	GOITER	EXHIBITION
PROSPEROUS	BRACE	HASTENS	FRET	HUSBANDRY
QUEER	GOAD	FREE SPACE	FESTER	BRACKEN
PROD	BLUNDERSOME	CORSET	YOKE	VAPORS
BARREN	SHANTIES	ROUSE	CLERGY	TRIBULATION

Day No Pigs Would Die Vocabulary

SILAGE	TRUNNEL	FARE	MIRTHFUL	TALONS
SPAR	QUIVERING	ASTIR	SLICKER	BROOD
CAPSTAN	SMARTED	FREE SPACE	MATTOCK	FEND
PARTIAL	COMELY	CORONER	MALLET	SUCCOTASH
PAUNCH	PROVOKED	CIPHER	STOUT	LOCO

Day No Pigs Would Die Vocabulary

POMADE	ROUSE	PROD	QUIVERING	GOAD
SMARTED	GOITER	SUCCOTASH	BLUNDERSOME	TRUNNEL
FRET	HASTENS	FREE SPACE	MALLET	COMELY
SHANTIES	BRACKEN	FEND	ASTIR	BROOD
PASSEL	ASTRIDE	SPAR	CIPHER	EXHIBITION

Day No Pigs Would Die Vocabulary

HUSBANDRY	FESTER	STOUT	MUZZLE	FARE
CORONER	CLERGY	CORSET	BARREN	TRIBULATION
SLICKER	LOCO	FREE SPACE	MIRTHFUL	BRACE
YOKE	VAPORS	PROSPEROUS	QUEER	PROVOKED
TALONS	PARTIAL	VARMINTS	PAUNCH	CAPSTAN

Day No Pigs Would Die Vocabulary

SMARTED	BRACE	BARREN	QUIVERING	SLICKER
MALLET	SUCCOTASH	FRET	MATTOCK	CIPHER
GOAD	COMELY	FREE SPACE	CAPSTAN	TRUNNEL
CORONER	BLUNDERSOME	BROOD	ASTIR	HASTENS
MIRTHFUL	ASTRIDE	GOITER	LOCO	PROD

Day No Pigs Would Die Vocabulary

TALONS	POMADE	PAUNCH	SHANTIES	PASSEL
YOKE	STOUT	SILAGE	FEND	VAPORS
PROVOKED	FESTER	FREE SPACE	TRIBULATION	PROSPEROUS
PARTIAL	QUEER	FARE	ROUSE	SPAR
HUSBANDRY	CLERGY	CORSET	EXHIBITION	VARMINTS

Day No Pigs Would Die Vocabulary

CIPHER	MATTOCK	SHANTIES	MIRTHFUL	BLUNDERSOME
PAUNCH	LOCO	VAPORS	SPAR	CAPSTAN
PROVOKED	BRACKEN	FREE SPACE	ASTIR	FARE
QUEER	CORONER	TRUNNEL	PROD	MALLET
ROUSE	STOUT	BROOD	ASTRIDE	PARTIAL

Day No Pigs Would Die Vocabulary

PASSEL	TRIBULATION	HASTENS	BARREN	SLICKER
TALONS	YOKE	BRACE	FEND	POMADE
MUZZLE	HUSBANDRY	FREE SPACE	QUIVERING	SMARTED
GOAD	SUCCOTASH	FESTER	SILAGE	CORSET
CLERGY	EXHIBITION	PROSPEROUS	COMELY	FRET

Day No Pigs Would Die Vocabulary

HASTENS	TRUNNEL	CAPSTAN	SLICKER	SHANTIES
CORONER	TRIBULATION	BRACKEN	SPAR	QUIVERING
BROOD	SMARTED	FREE SPACE	ASTIR	PAUNCH
MIRTHFUL	MATTOCK	CLERGY	COMELY	GOITER
LOCO	ROUSE	CIPHER	PROSPEROUS	PROVOKED

Day No Pigs Would Die Vocabulary

BLUNDERSOME	EXHIBITION	STOUT	FARE	VARMINTS
TALONS	SUCCOTASH	VAPORS	QUEER	SILAGE
FESTER	ASTRIDE	FREE SPACE	HUSBANDRY	BRACE
MUZZLE	FEND	GOAD	PROD	BARREN
YOKE	POMADE	PASSEL	CORSET	FRET

Day No Pigs Would Die Vocabulary

HASTENS	CORONER	TALONS	QUIVERING	MUZZLE
BARREN	FRET	CLERGY	PROD	QUEER
PROSPEROUS	COMELY	FREE SPACE	MIRTHFUL	BROOD
PARTIAL	BLUNDERSOME	PAUNCH	FEND	VARMINTS
EXHIBITION	CAPSTAN	PROVOKED	ROUSE	CORSET

Day No Pigs Would Die Vocabulary

SHANTIES	HUSBANDRY	STOUT	TRIBULATION	LOCO
VAPORS	GOAD	SMARTED	FESTER	MATTOCK
SUCCOTASH	BRACE	FREE SPACE	CIPHER	TRUNNEL
PASSEL	MALLET	ASTIR	SPAR	ASTRIDE
FARE	BRACKEN	SLICKER	SILAGE	GOITER

www.ingramcontent.com/pod-product-compliance
Lightning Source LLC
Chambersburg PA
CBHW081455070526
44586CB00019B/2369